Diary of a Victorian Miss on Holiday

Edited by
Helen and Keith Kelsall

Marie, aged 21, and her three brothers. Standing on the left is Howard, just 10, and on the right Richard Stuart, 16; Norman Hill (seated) is just 14. Taken in Birmingham in late 1887, the year of the diary.

Diary of a Victorian Miss on Holiday

Edited by
Helen and Keith Kelsall

The **Hallamshire** Press
1992

Published by The Hallamshire Press
The Hallamshire Press is an imprint of
Interleaf Productions Limited
Exchange Works
Sidney Street
Sheffield S1 3QF
England

Typeset by Interleaf Productions Limited
and
Printed in Great Britain
by The Cromwell Press
Wiltshire

British Library Cataloguing in Publication Data

Diary of a Victorian Miss on Holiday
I. Kelsall, Helen M. II. Kelsall, R.K.
941.081092

ISBN 1-874718-00-8

CONTENTS

LIST OF ILLUSTRATIONS

ACKNOWLEDGEMENTS

Special acknowledgement must be made of the tireless efforts and enthusiasm of Eric Rolls, a fellow Glasgow University Graduate now living in Birmingham, without which the painstaking research needed might often have ground to a halt.

The kindness and hospitality of the Headmistress and Archivist at the North London Collegiate School, who allowed access to their records, was of very great assistance.

All Marie's relatives with whom contact was made were most co-operative. They included Mr Arthur Stuart Todd in Australia, Mrs Dorothea Eyre in West Sussex, and above all Mrs Stella Mary Panton in Malvern and Mrs Elizabeth Ann Gibson in Woking, whose help in providing photo-graphs, guidance and encouragement was absolutely invaluable.

And last, but by no means least, grateful thanks to Pauline Climpson, Mark Glover, and the staff of Interleaf Productions Limited for showing their customary patience and forbearance.

I

INTRODUCTION

I

INTRODUCTION

(1) *How the manuscript was found, and why it was decided to publish it*

The manuscript holiday diary and scrapbook of Marie Todd was found among a barrow-load of second-hand books in a Birmingham back street in the mid-1940s. It had all the appearance of a normal cloth-bound printed book, its title on the cover being *My Holiday*: *A Record in Pen and Pencil*, the publisher John F. Shaw and Co., 48 Paternoster Row, London. Inside were about two dozen pages, many with printed floral decorations and short quotations from poems, some containing a blank circle or rectangle in which to paste a holiday memento. Four pages had no decoration but were headed 'Ferns and Leaves', 'Grasses', 'Wild Flowers' and 'Seaweed' respectively; another had the heading 'Autographs of People I Met'; others were for no specified use. And a special batch of green paper, thinner pages, was reserved for 'My Diary'.

So Marie Todd—whoever she was—had bought or been given a book in which to keep a record of a holiday, and had decided to use it for the *six* holidays she in fact had in 1887, the year of Queen Victoria's Jubilee. And apart from leaves, sprigs of heather, a few feathers and some standard photographs of well-known places, everything else she included in this record of her holidays has been faithfully reproduced here exactly as it was in 1887—pencil sketches, autographs, lists of places visited and events attended and, above all, the diary she wrote every day, the writing becoming darker after each dip of her steel pen into the inkwell. It brings to life, as nothing else could, what it was like to live in Britain then if you were the 21-year-old daughter of fairly well-to-do Birmingham parents. We learn what happened to this girl every day, written down that very evening or the following morning, what she did, whom she met, and what she thought about it all.

But what, it may be asked, is the value of something of this kind produced by someone unknown outside her own circle of family and friends?

To begin with, because diaries, along with letters, form a unique type of historical source which other records cannot match, to add even one to their number is well worth doing. For a girl or a woman to keep a journal in the nineteenth century was not, it is true, all that unusual; the Queen herself led the way. But, as in her case, diaries were often simply part of the upbringing process, to be carefully scrutinised by an elder. (Marie Todd's certainly does not fall into *that* category.) And in any event, it was not normally thought to be worth publishing one unless its keeper had some claim on the attention of potential readers.

Such a claim might arise in a variety of ways. If Anne Jemima Clough had not afterwards become the first Principal of Newnham; if Margaret Dyne Jeune had not known everyone of importance in Oxford and been the wife of the Master of Pembroke; if Ada Louise Hammond had not happened to be an aunt of the well-known playwright Christopher Fry; and but for the sheer scholarship shown by Emily Shore, it is safe to say that none of *their* diaries would ever have reached a wider public than a small circle of relatives and close friends.

There is, however, one notable exception to this general rule that nineteenth-century women's diaries are only published if the journal-keeper is herself well known (or later becomes so), if she is connected with some public figure, or if she displays specialised knowledge and skill in some field. The exception is Ellen Weeton, a Lancashire lass of no particular distinction. But in her case, Edward Hall thought that the insight her journal and letters provided into the life of a governess, and into the hardships of downtrodden middle-class women generally, would justify their publication, which took place in 1936 and again in 1939. The very great interest aroused led to their being reprinted in 1969, along with other manuscript material, in the two-volume *Miss Weeton's Journal of a Governess 1807–25*.

There was certainly nothing downtrodden about Marie Todd, but neither did she fulfil any of the other criteria that should make a journal of hers worthy of being put before a wide audience. It does not exhibit exceptional talents or knowledge, Marie herself neither started her adult life as, nor became, a notable figure in her own right, nor were any of those with whom she was closely connected nationally well known. So her diary epitomises the hundreds of others that must have been lost or thrown away because they, and those who kept them, lacked the particular kinds of distinction that had become the accepted criteria without which publication was not thought to be warranted.

One can only hope that now, in the 1990s, the realisation of the irreparable loss we have all suffered as a result of the rigid application of these criteria will lead people to welcome the salvaging of any of these diaries that have escaped destruction.

In terms of the age of the diarist, and of the relatively short span of time covered by her efforts, probably the nearest nineteenth-century equivalents to the present diary (though both are over fifty years earlier in date) are those of Anne Chalmers and Georgina Smythe. The similarity in the first of these cases is that Anne Chalmers (daughter of the famous Dr Chalmers, Professor of Divinity at Edinburgh University) kept a diary at the age of 17 for only ten weeks or so when visiting London with her father and mother in 1830; publication took place in 1923. Mrs Fitzherbert's niece, Georgina Smythe, at 18 and 19, kept one for part of the years 1832 and 1833, but here the interest lies in forming part of a love story (quite unlike Marie's holiday diary), so that her journal, along with the longer one (1827–31) of her elder sister Louisa, became the centrepiece of Richard Buckle's *The Prettiest Girl in England* (1958).

Granted, then, that a diary can bring vividly to life what it was like to be a certain age, and to live in a particular social and geographical setting at a specific time, what is so special about 1887? Not merely that it is now more than a century ago, but also that it was a time of particularly interesting transition and contrast between the old and the new, which affected almost every aspect of daily life.

Take the business of travelling around the country, particularly important on holiday. The diary lets us see what it was like to live in a period combining old and new forms of transport. Old-fashioned horse-drawn vehicles of every description were in use as there were no cars (pneumatic tyres for bicycles and other vehicles were not brought out by Dunlop until 1888), and these existed alongside modern steamers and steam trains, the latter running on a much more extensive network of railways than we have today. (So many of the branch lines, including several that Marie used, have been eliminated by Beeching and others.) And where else could we get such colourful detail to bring it all to life as knowing how long the journeys actually took, how in certain areas (e.g. the Highland Railway) trains had the reputation of being habitually late, or that on a long journey a fellow passenger in your compartment might produce 'a little stove and all complete' and have 'a little cooking performance'?

Or take the question of communicating with friends and relatives. If you wanted to keep in touch you still had, as had always been the case, to write long letters at frequent intervals, as the diary tells us Marie habitually did. Yet this old-fashioned situation was already on the way out, for in 1887 it existed alongside a growing network of telegrams and telephones. Post Office telegrams were being sent as early as 1870, and telegram facilities had already been provided by a number of companies (including railway companies) for several years before this. The great upsurge in their use only took place, however, after the Post Office minimum charge had been reduced from a shilling to sixpence. This happened less than two years before Marie's brothers sent their telegram from Birmingham to greet her and their parents on arrival in Glasgow, where it reached them remarkably quickly in its familiar red envelope and was carefully pasted into her holiday album. Ingenuity enabled you to qualify for the sixpenny tariff by keeping the address and the message to no more than twelve words (extra words cost a halfpenny each). By 1887 some five million telegrams were being sent annually in the UK.

Telephones came somewhat later. But once Sir William Thompson had demonstrated Graham Bell's invention at the British Association Meeting in Glasgow in September 1878, things moved forward fairly rapidly. Yet Marie Todd, nine years later, makes no actual mention of having spoken on the telephone during any of her holidays; a nationwide system, in the hands by then of the National Telephone Company and the Post Office, did not really begin to take shape until the 1890s.

Then again, as we all know, before the coming of radio and television, of videos and tape-recorders, and when even gramophones were not yet available, people had to make their own entertainment in the evenings, whether at home or on holiday in boarding houses and hotels. And in a diary such as Marie's we see this in action; we can almost hear the banjo being strummed, the songs being sung, the buzz of conversation, and the participation of virtually everyone in some of these activities, no one feeling inhibited from taking part by lack of talent, or worrying unduly about the *quality* of what was produced by their joint efforts. Thus, although Marie obviously found great pleasure in listening, for instance, to the excellent violin or organ playing of good amateurs such as her friends Bertram Fletcher in Cambridge or Percy Buck in West Ham, she nowhere tells us of her distress or disappointment at the many *poor* performances by amateurs she must have listened to—this was just part of life, and you accepted it with as good a grace as you could muster. And you glowed with pleasure, as she did, when some of your own efforts (on the banjo, for instance) were appreciated at these informal gatherings.

Looking at another aspect of life, in the days before the Number 2 Brownie box camera, only a few keen and experienced photographers took a camera and tripod with them on holiday. Otherwise, as Marie did, you had to try your hand at pencil sketches of people and places, or at painting in water colours or oils, however much you were aware (as she was) of the feebleness of your efforts. But there were at least some photos to be bought that could be pasted into your album to supplement what you yourself had been able to achieve by more old-fashioned means. There were also, of course, visits to the photographer's studio. And one great advantage of a late, compared with an early nineteenth-century diary, is that of being able, for the first time, to include a photo of the diarist at the actual time she was writing it, as we have been able to do in the present case. Not only Marie herself, but also her mother and her three brothers can be seen as they were in the diary year, 1887. This added interest of knowing what the writer and some of the others mentioned in the diary actually looked like at the relevant time is not provided in the published journals of Miss Weeton (1807–25), Miss Clough (1837–49), Miss Shore (1831–39) and Mrs Jeune (1843–62), all of which—except the last—were written before the benefits of photography became generally available. The difference it can make to one's enjoyment and understanding is clearly demonstrated by the case of the girl from Chicago, Julia Newberry, whose published diary (1867–71) includes an excellent studio photograph revealing her character and temperament to an astonishing degree. But one of the nineteenth-century Englishwomen, extracts from whose journal (1838–73) have probably derived the greatest benefit from being accompanied by a number of photographs and portraits of the principal characters, is Mrs Caroline Clive; her great-grandson's widow, Mary Clive, was able to assemble almost a dozen such illustrations for the book that appeared in 1949. Another case where it has been of enormous benefit to have photographs of many of the people concerned is that of Ada Louise Hammond. The diary of his Aunt Ada, spanning more than half a century (1869–1920), formed the fascinating central thread of Christopher Fry's family history, *Can You Find Me?* (1978).

Finally, although 1887 may, in retrospect, seem to have been a relatively tranquil year in Britain's history, it is worth remembering that British trade had been going through a recession, evidenced by what happened after a meeting in Trafalgar Square the previous February, when a mob of the unemployed engaged in quite extensive window-smashing and looting of shops in Pall Mall, Piccadilly and South Audley Street. The diary notes that industrial unrest caused minor disruption to one of Marie's many train journeys in 1887—'got home much late owing to the strike of the Midland men' (Friday 5th August).

We may have up to now given a somewhat exaggerated impression of the *ordinariness* of Marie's diary. Yet she was lucky in several important respects, and *her* good fortune was *our* good fortune as well. First of all, being the daughter of well-to-do parents she could afford to have six holidays in one year—with friends in a wide variety of places in England (among farmers in the Tamworth area, stately homes on the Leicestershire–Derbyshire borders, in Cambridge, and in London), and with her mother and father on an extensive tour of Scotland taking them up to the Highlands. And secondly, by another piece of good fortune, her father had sent her, as a boarder, to a school that was in the forefront of the nineteenth-century movement to improve the education of women, the North London Collegiate School for Girls, where she stayed in the house of the Headmistress, the famous Miss Buss. Having been kindly given access to their archives, it has been possible to say a good deal about her life as a schoolgirl there, to supplement what she herself tells us in her diary about her return to Myra Lodge on holiday in 1887.

(2) *What background material was needed*

A diary may be, as we have claimed, a unique source for gaining an impression of what life was like in a particular social setting in a given place at a specific time. But to appreciate it to the full, and to gain the maximum benefit from it, we need supplementary information of at least three or four kinds. First, the background of the diarist himself or herself, in this case something about her family of origin and her schooldays. Secondly, it is certainly helpful and interesting to know what happened afterwards—in Marie's case when she got married and to whom, and some material on her husband's background, leading on to the family the two of them established together, and ultimately to someone (and there are, sadly, very few such people still living) who actually remembers her, at least in her later years.

Thirdly, a commentary is needed to provide the necessary explanations of the people, places and other matters mentioned in the diary, the significance of which is not, a century afterwards, immediately clear without some elucidation. Fourthly and finally—a section that can easily be skipped by those not interested—a brief sketch can be given of the methods employed and sources used in tracing and making contact with any surviving descendants of Marie. From the diary itself, as can be seen, all that could be gleaned about Marie Todd was that she lived in Calthorpe Road, Birmingham, had a father, R.F. Todd, who was part-owner of a flour mill, and had apparently as a schoolgirl boarded with a certain Miss Buss and others in a house in London called Myra Lodge. From that starting point to success in finding her only surviving grandchild took over nine months, with many blind alleys and disappointments on the way.

(3) *The search for surviving descendants*

So we can begin with this brief sketch of the nine-month search. Had this manuscript been passed from one generation of the family to the next, as would normally have happened, the task of discovering more about the diarist herself would have been a comparatively easy one. Due to Marie and her husband being bombed out of their house at 22 Somerset Road, Birmingham in the early part of the war, however, the diary turned up, as has been said, on a barrow of second-hand books, and so a lengthy search had to take place. The starting point was provided by the diary entry for Thursday 26th May: 'So very glad to see Calthorpe Road again'.

Without the *number* of the Calthorpe Road house, progress was going to be difficult, so the starting point had to be to look at local directories of Birmingham. These had been published annually for a large slice of the nineteenth, and the first half of the twentieth century by Kelly's and certain other publishers. Typically they included an alphabetical list, called 'private residents' or 'Court', as well as a street-by-street list of such people. From these lists one can discover roughly when a particular householder moved into, or left a particular house. And in the commercial section one can see when a business was started and when it disappeared. Having obtained the Calthorpe Road number—56—the next step was to examine the Decennial Population Census returns for that part of Birmingham. Under the hundred-year rule, the latest date for which the detailed enumerator's household returns could be consulted was 1881, the 1891 figures not being made available until about Easter 1992. When the 1881 census was taken, Marie Todd was not at 56 Calthorpe Road; it later transpired that she was with Miss Buss at Myra Lodge on that census night. But she was found at 56 Calthorpe Road in the 1871 census.

From then on it was a matter of finding dates of birth, marriage and death of Marie herself, her brothers, her husband and his brothers and sisters, and trying to discover what children they had and where they lived. Addresses, even when available, were always of course out of date; and as all the next generation (and some even of Marie's own generation) of both Todds and Lowes had moved away from Birmingham to unknown other parts of the country, local directories and telephone directories (the latter with the drawback of ex-directory or unlisted subscribers) proved of very little value at this stage.

Who's Who and *Who was Who* also yielded very little—just one of Marie's nephews who was an MP for a time, and one of Conway's brothers who had a distinguished law career, but that was all. *Landed Gentry* was equally unrewarding, but one of Marie's brothers who was High Sheriff of Worcestershire was listed there, together with a fairly full account of his father Richard Farmer Todd's descendants up to 1952, but limited to dates of birth, marriage and death. Registers of the schools known to have been attended by some of Marie's and Conway's brothers (and a few of the later generation) were also consulted, but very little information emerged that had not already been gleaned from other sources. Census returns for 1891 and all the following decades not being available, Electoral Registers were consulted. These, of course, only contained the names of those living at particular addresses who were entitled to vote, and added little to what had been discovered elsewhere.

So, in order to obtain the full names of Marie's children and grandchildren, nephews and nieces, grand-nephews and grand-nieces, the National Probate Index had to be consulted for dates of probate of the relevant Wills likely to contain these names. And then there began the lengthy task of trying to attach up-to-date addresses to these names in order to establish contact with some of her descendants. In the end, four people in particular were found: the widow of a grand-nephew, another grand-nephew living in Australia, the widow of her grandson, and her only grand-daughter, all of whom have proved extremely helpful.

Having given this brief sketch of the nine-month search, we can give an account of Marie's life *before* she wrote the diary, and later go on to say what happened to her afterwards—her marriage, her husband's family, the family they established together, and what became of her three brothers. But first, a family tree and family photographs can be provided.

II

A FAMILY TREE, AND FAMILY PHOTOGRAPHS

Marie is shown at various ages between 21 and 73. Also shown are her mother, her father, her three brothers, her husband and their four children, taken while they were still children.

Family Tree showing the children, grandchildren and great-grandchildren of Richard Farmer Todd and Mary Hill

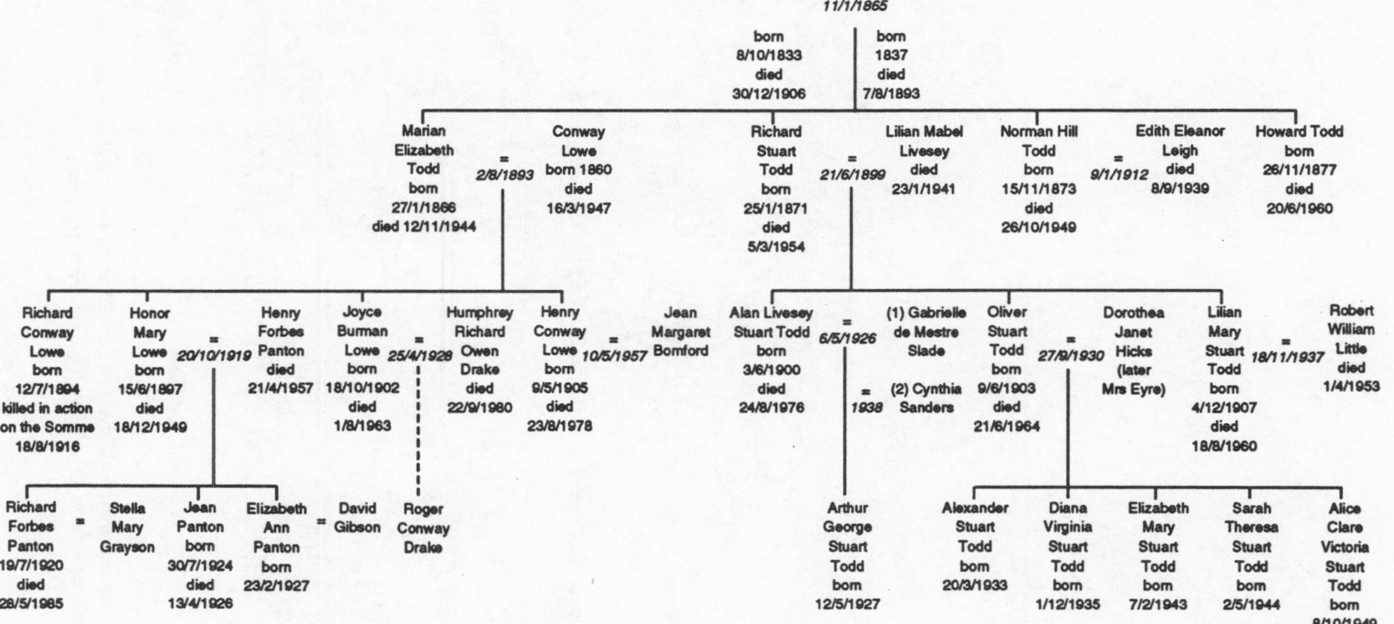

Marie (standing), aged 21, and her mother (seated), aged 50, taken in Birmingham, July 7th 1887, the year of the diary.

Marie, aged 21, and her three brothers. Standing on the left is Howard, just 10, and on the right Richard Stuart, 16; Norman Hill (seated) is just 14. Taken in Birmingham in late 1887, the year of the diary.

Marie, aged 27, just before she married, taken in Birmingham in 1893.

Marie, aged 32, on the left in the front row; her brother Richard Stuart, 27, is second from the right in the back row. Taken on holiday in North Wales, probably in 1898.

From left to right: Marie's brother Norman Hill, aged 20; someone unknown; her father, aged 65; and her brother Richard Stuart, aged 27. Taken in Birmingham, probably in 1898.

Marie, aged 33, with her children Richard Conway Lowe, aged 5, and Honor Mary Lowe, aged 2. Taken in Birmingham in 1899.

Marie, aged 36, with her husband Conway Lowe, 42, and their children Richard Conway Lowe, 8, and Honor Mary Lowe, 5. Taken in Rhyl, probably in 1902.

Marie and Conway's children, Richard Conway Lowe, 10, Honor Mary Lowe, 7, and Joyce Burman Lowe, just over 1. Taken in Birmingham in 1904.

Marie's husband Conway Lowe, aged 45. Taken in Birmingham, Easter 1905.

The youngest of Marie and Conway's four children, Henry Conway Lowe (Darby), aged 8. Taken at Llanbedrog, probably in 1913.

Marie, aged 54. Taken on a visit to her brother Richard Stuart Todd at Clent Grove in August 1920.

Marie, aged 64. Taken in Birmingham, probably in 1930.

Marie, aged 73. Taken in the garden of 'Eversley', 22 Somerset Road, Birmingham, probably in 1939.

III

MARIE TODD BEFORE 1887

III

MARIE TODD BEFORE 1887

Marie, 21 when she wrote the diary in 1887, had lived at 56 Calthorpe Road, a modest semi-detached house a few doors from St George's Vicarage in Edgbaston, since she was a little girl. Her father was Richard Farmer Todd, 53, part-owner of a flour mill in Ladywood. He was a very tall man, of whom it was said that he kept his top hat on more than was usual to protect his head from hitting rafters and door frames at the mill and elsewhere. He was also heavily built, at one time weighing twenty-six stone. He had married Mary Hill from Coventry, who was now 50. Marie (christened Marian Elizabeth) was the first-born, followed five years later by Richard Stuart (always known simply as Stuart), then by Norman Hill, now 13, and finally by Howard, 9.

After having been a pupil for seven years at Mrs Rubery's school at 233 Hagley Road, Marie went as a boarder to the North London Collegiate School for Girls in 1880, when she was 14. This school was not merely an unusual choice for Marie's parents to make at that time, but a very wise decision both scholastically, for character training, and in every way. For the North London Collegiate, as Felicia Lamb says looking back on things from a 1968 vantage point, 'was outstanding among the dismal, useless, unhealthy schools that crowded the country . . . Fresh air was in, social and religious snobbishness was out.' It had become a model that was to be eagerly copied, ever since the Taunton Commission had recommended in 1869 that a school for girls on similar lines should be set up in every town in the country.

Perhaps one aspect of the school was open to serious criticism. For Miss Buss was insistent that the girls should abide by an ever-increasing set of rules, the breaking of any of which necessitated the culprit herself making an entry in the Appearing Book. Mrs M. Vivian Hughes (who, as Mary Thomas, was a pupil a year younger than Marie) was one of those who reacted adversely to these arrangements, as she recounts in

The house on the left is 56 Calthorpe Road, Edgbaston, Marie's home from early childhood until, aged 27, she married Conway Lowe in 1893. This photograph (courtesy of the Calthorpe Estate Office) was taken in 1969, the year in which the building was demolished.

A London Girl of the Eighties (1936). Marie may have felt the same way on this aspect of her schooling, for in her 1887 holiday diary on Thursday 19th May she 'walked in rain down to school and did not enjoy the sight thereof or the walk'. No doubt it brought all too vividly to mind many such walks from Myra to the school, almost inevitably in bad weather breaking the rule about having to arrive there dry. The bare statement of such a rule, of course, sounds harsh and even silly. But all it really meant was 'wrap up well, and when you get to school do everything necessary to avoid sitting around in damp clothes'. For wet days an extra pair of stockings had to be kept on one's peg in the cloakroom. And to quote Sara Burstall in *Frances Mary Buss* (1938): 'As a form mistress, one had, on wet days, to feel the skirts and stockings of one's girls so that they should not sit in wet things and get ill. The building provided open fires at which failures could remedy their fault, and there was in the basement a drying room where the outdoor garments could be dried before the end of the school day.'

However she may sometimes have felt when looking back on it, Marie's participation in school affairs seems to have won approval both from staff and fellow pupils. We know, for example, that she served as a monitor after having been in school for the required one year. Monitors were elected on the first day of the term, and to be eligible for election a girl must not have signed the Appearing Book more than ten times, or be below fifteenth in position in class. Once elected she attended the meetings where staff, monitors and prefects discussed what was needed to improve discipline. Then in her Prize Day Speech on July 3rd 1882, Miss Buss announced that the Platt Endowment Exhibitions of £10, awarded on the results of the Junior Cambridge Local Examination, had been gained by Marian E. Todd and Beatrice E.W. Buck (the Mabel Buck in the Diary). Marie was also commended on another occasion for her translation of a French poem into English verse; while in the School Prize List in 1883, her last year at the North London, she is mentioned for Scripture, English, Science and Languages.

It would have been nice to be able to reproduce a photograph of Marie when she was a schoolgirl, but unfortunately she cannot be identified in the group pictures amongst the North London archives, while no family photos prior to 1887 seem to have survived. All we can do is to give some very scant information gleaned from school medical inspection records. These tell us that in 1880, when Marie was 14, her height was 5ft 4ins, that a year later it was 5ft 6¼ins, and in November 1882, now aged 16¾, she had reached 5ft 8¼ins, obviously taking after her tall father. Her weight on that last occasion was 143lbs. Her hair was

276 Term III 1880

North London Collegiate School for Girls,

OFFICE—202, CAMDEN ROAD.

Fee for Registration of Application, Half-a-Crown.

APPLICATION FOR ADMISSION.

Christian Name, Surname, Age, and date of birth of the pupil, to be written in full.	Marian Elizabeth Todd aged fourteen Born January 27th 1866.
Profession or occupation of Father (if living) or Guardian.	Miller.
Has the pupil been to school before? If so, where, and how long?	Mrs Rubery. Edgbaston Birmingham. 6 3/4 years.

SIGNATURE OF REFEREE.

(1.) *To the Parent or Guardian of a pupil already in the School: or*
(2.) *To a Householder.*

I recommend Marian Elizabeth Todd.
for admission to the North London Collegiate School for Girls.

Signature in full Daniel M Grimshaw

Address Uxbridge

SIGNATURE OF FATHER (IF LIVING) OR GUARDIAN.

Name in full Richard. Farmer. Todd.

Address 56 Calthorpe. Road. Birmingham

If my daughter is admitted to the School, I hereby agree to abide by all the regulations made for the government of the School.

Signature of Father (if living) or Guardian R. F. Todd.

Date March 13th 1880.

Application for Marie Todd to be admitted to the North London Collegiate School for Girls

'No. 6' and her eyes 'light grey'. Her spine was straight, and both her heart and her lungs were sound. Her sight at twelve feet was perfect.

The North London Collegiate School for Girls in Sandall Road in the 1880s

Although the number of pupils in attendance at this time was around five hundred (excluding another eighty or so in preparatory classes), these were nearly all day pupils. Life for the handful of boarders at Myra Lodge was very different, and there can be no doubt at all that Marie thoroughly enjoyed her three years there. There are two reasons for believing this. The first is that she would never have wanted to spend part of her London holiday there four years later had this not been so. And secondly, when the time came for her to decide on a school for her own two daughters, she chose to send them as boarders to a predominantly day school run on very similar lines to the North London. By that time her old school had ceased to take any boarders, but Marie clearly felt that, from her own experience, to board with the headmistress was both beneficial and enjoyable. So as Miss Mary Wolseley-Lewis (someone of Marie's age, who had been a pupil and then a teacher at Miss Beale's Cheltenham College) had in 1909 started North Foreland Lodge in Broadstairs, Honor Mary was sent there as a boarder in 1912 (when she was 15) and became Head Girl before she left in 1915, while Joyce Burman followed her, also at 15, in 1917, leaving in 1919.

How much do we know of what life had been like for Marie at Myra Lodge? In her 1895 biography of Frances Mary Buss, Annie E. Ridley writes: 'In accordance with her own theories, she tried to make Myra Lodge as home-like as possible. And the welfare of her girls—physical, mental and spiritual—was her first care.' And Josephine Kamm in *How Different from Us* (1958) tells us that

> the Myra girls had an abundance of good-night kissing, good plain food, and special treats on half-term holidays and birthdays. Among the Myra girls' privileges was a walk to and from school unencumbered by a heavy satchel of books: on Miss Buss's instructions the satchels were piled on the roof of her four-wheeled cab.

Another old pupil writes, 'Miss Buss frequently gave parties at Myra Lodge to which she invited a considerable number of other girls in the school'. There was no school atmosphere about these parties, which included charades—anyone with any gift at all could take part. But at least one day pupil 'did not envy the Myra girls for the loose, warm clothing they had to wear or for the ban which Miss Buss had placed on tight-lacing and stiff stays'.

In the chorus of praise for what life was like for those who boarded with Miss Buss at Myra Lodge in the 1870s and 1880s there was, however, at least one discordant note which it would be wrong to ignore completely. A girl who left Myra in 1880, the year Marie arrived there, was Janet (called Netta) Syrett. Netta, who became a prolific novelist and writer of children's books and plays, gives a graphic and disturbing account of things in her autobiographical reminiscences, *The Sheltering Tree* (1939). She was 11 and her sister Dora only 10, and a few minutes after their father had left them at Myra they were 'seated on the floor of a bleak bedroom, crying bitterly'; but instead of any attempt at consolation, the woman who came to supervise their unpacking simply told them they were not allowed to talk in bedrooms because it was against the rules, and then left them without another word. Nor did things improve after that first evening. By Netta's account, constant and often violent rows took place with Miss Buss. 'To me, living in the same house with her was like breathing the electric atmosphere of an impending storm, which, all too frequently, broke.'

We learn more about what life, seen through Netta Syrett's eyes, was like at Myra Lodge in the 1880s by reading the account she gives in one of her early novels, *The Victorians* (1915). This is the story of the first part of the life of Rose Cottingham (Netta herself in many, but not all,

Frances Mary Buss in 1883

The gymnasium of the North London Collegiate School for Girls. From the Girls' Own Paper, *1882.*

essential respects). The section on her schooldays extends to some 166 out of a total of 384 pages; the fictional school she attended was clearly a close counterpart of the North London Collegiate, Miss Quayle was modelled on Miss Buss, Minerva House was Myra Lodge, and the sympathetic teacher Miss Mortlake was, as Netta afterwards tells us in her autobiography, Miss Fawcett; who the thoroughly unpleasant Miss Bird was in real life one cannot do more than guess, but she was obviously

Caroline Fawcett

the factotum who came to watch Netta and her sister unpacking on their first night away from home.

A typical example of how a violent storm would suddenly blow up at Minerva House is provided by the instance where Miss Quayle, returning from a long day's activity at school, would pay a surprise visit to the boot-lockers

> to assure herself that every boot was marked by its owner's name on the lining, and placed tidily on the shelf allotted to each pupil. She would dash open every drawer in a particular bedroom and, descending in a fury worthy of a more important cause, summon the whole household, reducing half of it to tears, and spreading general terror by the thunder of her eloquence and the scorching fire of her condemnation.

Some compensation was, it is true, provided when 'sometimes at supper-time the Principal read aloud, or with the older girls discussed a book of William Morris'; and then there were the very enjoyable outings to the theatre. Rose was the first to admit that Miss Quayle held liberal and advanced views on the independence of womankind, and that the social mix she provided by her admissions policy was highly beneficial; but none of this could excuse the flagrant unfairness, the refusal to listen to any explanation, the lack of any sense of proportion, and the rigidity of the discipline that was constantly imposed.

Whatever uncertainty may exist about the authenticity of some (but not all) of the events described in Netta Syrett's novel, there is at least no doubt about the factual details in the enumerator's 1881 census return of those living at Myra Lodge. There were twenty-two girls besides Marie herself described as 'scholars', their ages ranging from 14 to 18. If we take birthplace as a possible guide to where their homes were, two were from overseas (India and Australia), one from Scotland (Glasgow), seven from the North and Midlands, four from the South, and the remaining eight from London and the Home Counties (including Marie's friend Mabel Buck). Apart from five domestic servants, the balance of the thirty-three people living there was made up by Miss Buss herself and five teachers—including her 43-year-old cousin Sarah Ann Paul (whose sumptuous lunch Marie felt greedy about enjoying—see her diary entry for May 18th), 22-year-old Miss Mary Bennett ('very kind and helpful to new girls, and an interesting teacher') and Miss Caroline Fawcett, 36 (no relation of Dame Millicent Fawcett: she and her husband Professor Fawcett only had one child, Philippa, who afterwards distinguished herself in mathematics).

As Caroline Fawcett was, without a shadow of doubt, Marie's all-time favourite on the staff (on revisiting Myra Lodge in 1887, 42-year-old Miss Fawcett was her constant companion on shopping expeditions, evening excursions, and making music together in the drawing room), no excuse is needed for providing as much information as possible about her. To begin with, it is clear that she was not only Marie's favourite, but everyone else's as well. Isabel Monkhouse, for instance (who left school in 1894 and was on the staff for twenty-seven years), says: 'many members of the staff will never be forgotten. Miss Fawcett, mistress of Form 1, her smooth parted hair, thin long face, heavily lidded eyes and lips pressed together, very kind and gentle.' And Netta Syrett contrasts her unhappy memories of the rest of the Myra staff with 'the nice old housekeeper Miss Paul' and 'the kindly, human Miss Fawcett' (who often interceded for her during the progress of 'a row'). As we have already seen, she tells us that the understanding teacher, Miss Mortlake, in her fictional account of a Victorian School was in fact Miss Fawcett. She also says:

> That I made no effort to see Miss Fawcett after I was grown up, is one of the many sins of omission that trouble my conscience . . . I can only hope that if she read my early novel she recognised herself in the sympathetic mistress.

Unfortunately, just months before the novel was published, Caroline Fawcett had died.

Annie E. Ridley's 1895 biography of Miss Buss speaks (on page 336) of 'Miss Fawcett's Diary during her residence at Myra (1868–88)' and quotes from it occasionally. This would clearly be an invaluable source of information both about the diarist herself and about life at Myra; but no one today seems to have any idea where it now is, or how it might be tracked down. Marie herself would obviously have known that someone she so much admired was a diary-keeper, and indeed this may well have provided some of the inspiration for her own much more limited efforts in that direction. A sad sequel to all this is provided by the fact that Miss Annie Ridley, no doubt because of the great help Caroline Fawcett's diary had been to her when she was writing the Frances Mary Buss biography, decided when making her will in 1912 to provide an annuity of £100 for Caroline (which was about the equivalent of her salary as a teacher before she retired). But Miss Fawcett unfortunately never derived any benefit from this generous provision (and probably never even knew it had been made), as in the event Miss Ridley outlived her by some ten years.

So Caroline Fawcett, born in 1845, having become a member of staff when she was only 17 years old, retired from teaching in 1901 at 56, having given up her work at Myra some years before that. She only had thirteen years of retirement, and when she died was sharing a house at 25 Halifax Road, Cambridge with one of her sisters, Maria Fanny Fawcett. Because she was for so many years in charge of the youngest form at school, and because of her work as House Mistress at Myra

Lodge, generation after generation of North London girls came under her benign influence.

Perhaps if her diary is eventually located and published, as it should be, her true worth and the value of what she achieved will come to be appreciated by an even wider public than the comparatively limited circle of North Londoners to whom she gave a lifetime of such dedicated service.

IV

MARIE'S 1887 MANUSCRIPT

ye yeare of Jubilee 1887.

My Holidays.
during 1887.
at

Cambridge. May. 6th.
London. May. 10th.
Cambridge. June. 14th.
Comberford. July 19th.
Langley Priory. July 30th.
Scotland. Aug. 8th.

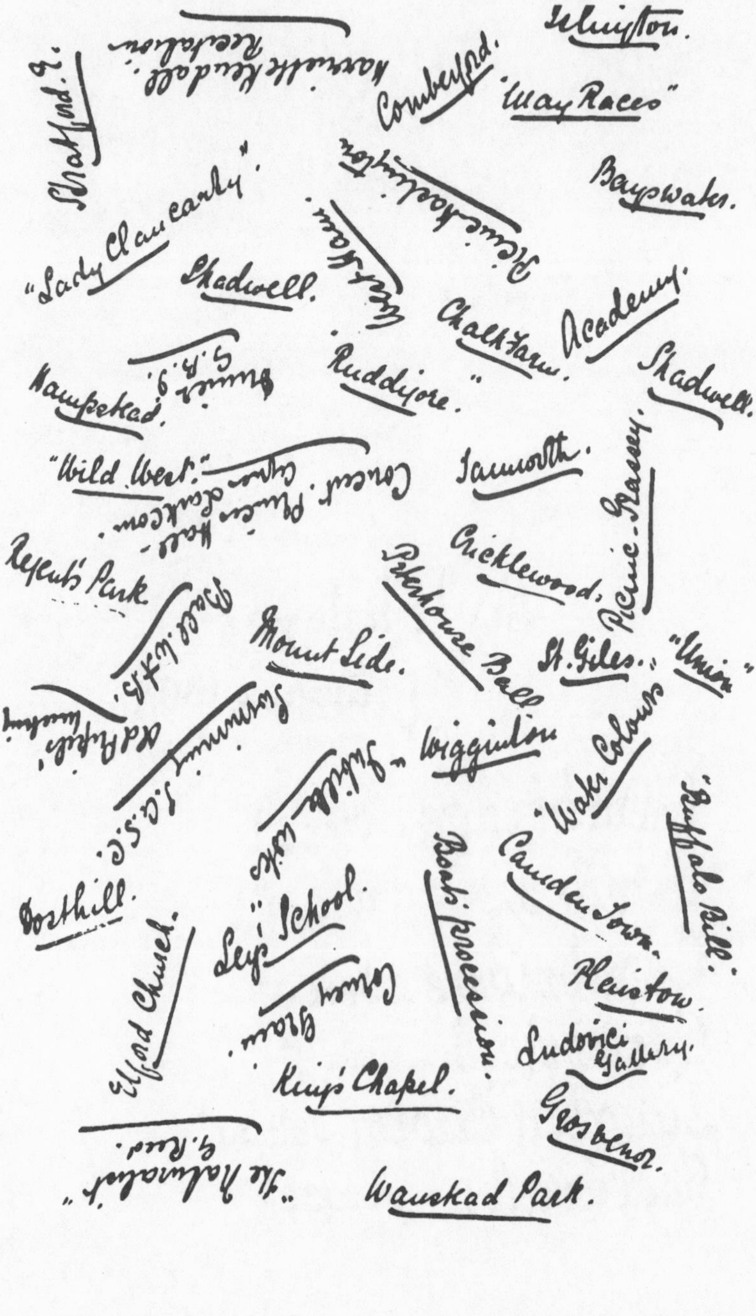

Islington.

"May Races"

Cumberland.

Stratford, E.

[illegible] Recitation

Bayswater.

"Lady Clancarty".

Kensington

Shadwell.

West Ham

Academy.

Chalk Farm.

Shadwell.

Hampstead.

S.R.G.

Ruddigore."

"Wild West."

Concert. Music Hall

Tamworth.

Picnic. Brassey.

Cricklewood.

Regent's Park

Peterhouse Ball

Mount Side.

St. Giles."

"Union"

Wigginton

"Water Colours

"Buffalo Bill."

Swimming S.C.S.C.

Jubilee

Dosthill.

Leys' School.

Camden Town.

Boat procession.

Plaistow.

Ludovici Gallery.

Oxford Church.

King's Chapel.

Grosvenor.

Hampstead Park.

"The [illegible]" G. Reed.

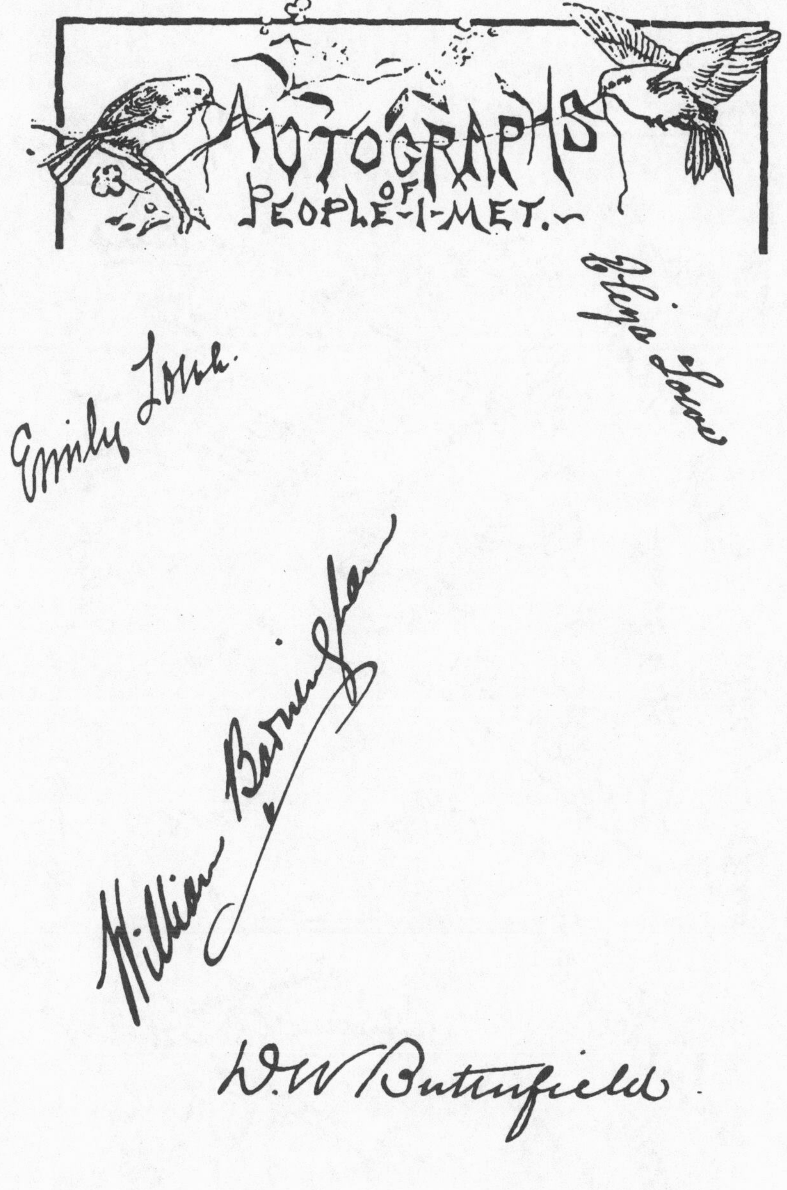

Florence E. Lowe

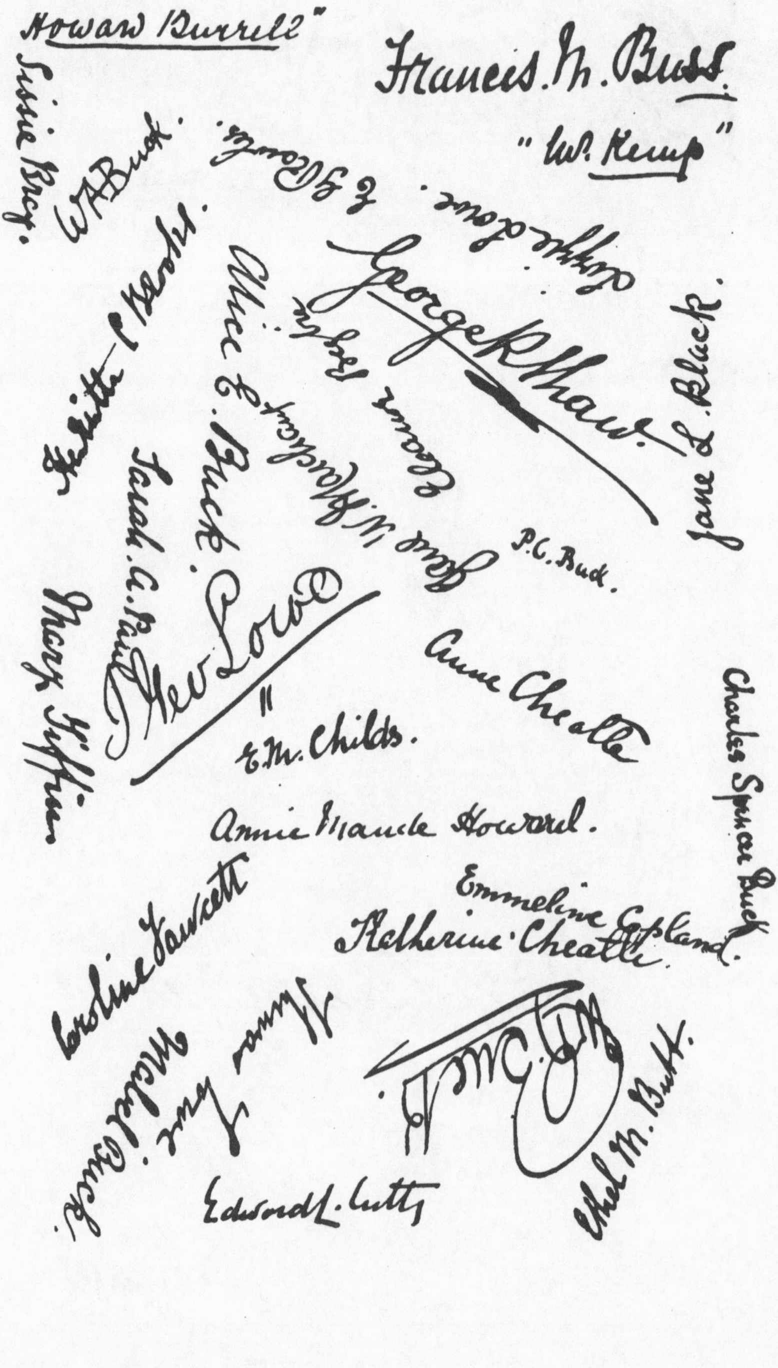

Howard Burrell

Frances M. Buss.

"W. Kemp"

Sissie Bray.

W. A. Buck.

George R. Shaw.

Jane S. Black.

Alice E. Buck.

P. C. Buck.

Anne Cheatle

E. M. Childs.

Charles Spencer Buck.

Annie Maude Howard.

Emmeline Copland.

Katherine Cheatle.

Caroline Fawcett

Mabel Buck.

Ethel M. Butt.

Edward L. Cutts

Stewarts-

Milray. Walford. "Bounder".

Arthur Buss. Walter Howard.

Rev. E. Bray.

Marian Lewis. Pearce. C. Coxon.

Miss Norris.

Wm. Franks

W. Sykes. Frances Parsons.

Papa Burrell. S. Bray.
London. "Widow"
Wm. Thompson.
Yorkshire. Mallynson.

Turner.

London.

W. Norris.

Wm. Franks.

Branscombe.

Fletcher.

Beckenham

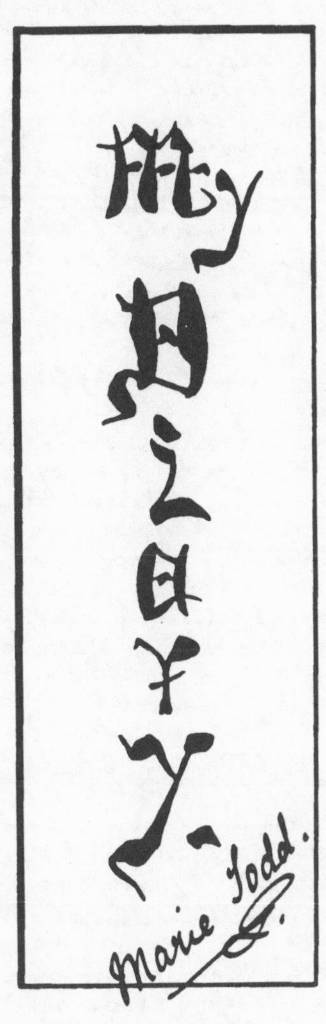

Including –
West Ham House.
Cambridge.
Quay Side.
Shadwell Rectory.
"Myra Lodge."
"Oaklands."
Comberford.
Langley Priory

Scotland –
Glasgow.
Oban.
Gairloch.
Inverness.
Fort William
Dunkeld. 1.
Braemar.
Dunkeld. 2.
Trossachs.
Edinburgh –

Thurs. May 5th

Tillie Rider's wedding day. Did not go to wedding as I originally intended owing to travelling involved. Mother started me by 12.45 to Euston. A carriage full of females – Changed at Willesden into Broad St train. Again at Broad St. & after much delay with luggage & porters I got over to Liverpool St. Took train for Stratford & arrived at West Ham about 4.0 Evidently much earlier than I was expected. After tea Mabel, Percy & I went to an amusing Concert at Plaistow. All amateurs, & some very queer ones. Walked there & back. Went to bed pretty well tired out.

Friday. May 6th Packed my own affairs & then had the pleasure of watching Mabel's skirmishes – assisting occasionally & wondering if ever we should get off in time for 11½ train. Finally accomplished this & eventually met Maude Howard at Liverpool St & started en route for Cambridge. Mrs Peck, Mabel, Maude & I. Arrived there during a downpour & found Willie to meet us in "Whites". Drove straight to our rooms & unpacked & then went to Willie's rooms & later Branscombe's to lunch. Owing to rain we all sat indoors after lunch, music & talking – nothing else to do. Service at King's at 5.0. Most glorious place. Then followed a rush – only one hour barely, to dress for the dance & everything upside down. Vehicle of course was punctual, we most unpunctual. Mabel in many difficulties. Dance at rooms in St Andrew's St. Got there soon after 7.0. After disrobing – trotted in Miss Peck's wake to dancing room. Introductions followed & then proceedings commenced. Programme got full to about 12 extras. I was lucky running at first just one man. Partners – Fletcher of Peterhouse – Blake Clare – Willie – Wallman Sidney – Burns (Laurie) – Norris – Mathieson – Barberry – Kirkham –

Thurs. May 5th
Lillie Rider's wedding day. Did not go to wedding as I originally intended owing to travelling involved. Mother started me by 12.45 to Euston. A carriage full of females - changed at Willesden into Broad St train. Again at Broad St. & after much delay with luggage a porter & I got over to Liverpool St. Took train for Stratford & arrived at West Ham about 4.0 evidently much earlier than I was expected. After tea Mabel, Percy & I went to an amusing concert at Plaistow. All amateurs, & some very queer ones. Walked there & back. Went to bed pretty well tired out.

Friday May 6th Packed my own affairs & then had the pleasure of watching terrible skirmishes - assisting occasionally & wondering if ever we should get off in time for the train. Finally accomplished this & eventually met Maude Howard at Liverpool St & started en route for Cambridge. Mrs Buck, Mabel, Maude & I. Arrived there during a downpour & found Willie to meet us in "whites". Drove straight to our rooms & unpacked & then went to Willie's rooms or rather Branscombe's to lunch. Owing to rain we all sat indoors after lunch. Music & talking - nothing else to do. Service at King's at 5.0. Most glorious place. Then followed a rush - only one hour, barely, to dress for the dance & everything upside down. Vehicle of course was punctual, we most unpunctual. Mabel in many difficulties. Dance at rooms in St Andrew's St. Got there soon after 7.0. After disrobing - trotted in Miss Buss' wake to dancing room. Introductions followed & then proceedings commenced. Programme got full to about 12 extras. I was lucky know ing at first just one man. Partners - Fletcher of Peterhouse – Drake Clare = Willie = Mallinson Sidney ≡ Buss (Laurie) = Norris ≡ Mathieson – Barbury – Kirkham –

enjoyed it so much – It ended as all nice things do only too soon, & we four females packed in & went home to our rooms in sadness.

Saturday. May 7th.

Woke early, considering the miles we had danced overnight – Willie came for us, & we breakfasted in Branscombe's rooms. Then hey for the Cam. Divided into two parties – Turner & Arthur Byss with the others – Mrs Buck, Maude, Willie & I together. Rowed a long way past Dillon, Maude & I principally. I rowed so effectually that I could eventually wear no gloves. Lunch with Willie & Branscombe. In afternoon – Willie took Maude & me all round everywhere – the "backs" – Colleges, river etc – finally meeting others at Kings & went to service there. Tea with Willie, then he, Mabel, Maude & I scampered off to the station to start Miss Buss; she had quite an ovation. Arthur Buss & 2 others to see her off. They came home with us. We called at Pooles rooms, & then home. Mabel, Willie & I went out again shopping, & wound up this jolly day by doing the backs by moonlight. Home to rooms. Heard "the place where the old horse died" through a window.

Sunday. May 8th.

Mrs Buck, Maude & I met Willie & went to early service at St. Giles. Very high. Branscombe there. Lovely morning. Breakfast in Branscombe's rooms. Then lovely walk round backs & to chapel at Kings. Again walked to Girton après – oh so hot! Theological conversation. Miss Ainsley & a don took us all over & round, saw Mary Mathieson's room the prettiest in the College. Walked back again. Dinner in [illegible]'s rooms. Sat round window after. Then to afternoon service at Kings. Splendid

Enjoyed it so much - it ended as all
nice things do only too soon, and we four
females packed in & went home to our
rooms in sadness.

Saturday May 7th

Woke early, considering the miles we had danced overnight - Willie came for us, & we breakfasted in Branscombe's rooms. Then hey for the Cam. Divided into two parties - Turner & Arthur Buss with the others - Mrs Buck, Maude, Willie & I together. Rowed a long way past Ditton, Maude & I principally - I rowed so effectually that I could eventually wear no gloves. Lunch with Willie & Branscombe. In afternoon, Willie took Maude & me all round everywhere - the "backs" - colleges, river etc - finally met the others at Kings & went to service there. Tea with Willie, then he, Mabel, Maude & I scampered off to the station to start Miss Buss; she had quite an ovation, Arthur Buss & 2 others to see her off. They came home with us. We called at Poole's rooms, & then home. Mabel, Willie & I went out again shopping & wound up this jolly day by doing the backs by moonlight. Home to rooms, heard "The place where the old horse died" through a window.

Sunday May 8th

Mrs Buck, Maude & I met Willie & went to early service at St. Giles. Very high. Branscombe there. Lovely morning. Breakfast in Branscombe's rooms. Then lovely walk round backs & to Chapel at Kings - Again. Walked to Girton - après - oh so hot! Theological conversation. Miss Anelay a don took us all over & round. Saw Mary Mathieson's room the prettiest in the College. Walked back again. Dinner in Willie's rooms. Sat round window after. Then to afternoon service at Kings. Splendid nato. Having the Dean asked us to tea but unfortunately we had another Engagement. Went straight to Arthur Buss' rooms & had tea with him. Two friends there. Hancock & — . Little A. B. made splendid host. All went walk afterwards, Willie to Hall. Met Branscombe at Johns. Had splendid seats there for service at End. I was next to the Vice Chancellor. Afterwards walked about Johns, till Willie met us. Then walked all about backs & Colleges. Branscombe took Mrs Buck home. Mabel & Maude went off to the Trinity Church, & Willie & I went round the backs again & then home. At 8.30. our "Musical Evening" began — Fletcher of Peterhouse & his brother with his violin — Pearce a tenor — Barton pianist — Tattam tenor. Had some splendid music. Branscombe also sang. After they had gone had more music by ourselves. Then finished up with Evening Hymn & they took us home.

Monday May 9th.

The Angelus woke me at 6.0. Got up & packed entirely before the rest got up. Breakfast at Willie's rooms. After breakfast went round Cambridge — then Willie had lecture — & Mrs Buck took us round the Colleges. did Union previously. Then Peterhouse (Fletcher's man) Pembroke — Corpus. St. Catherines — King's — Queens — Caius etc. Conor + viced. Home to lunch at Branscombe's rooms. Afterwards had a little dore — being so tired with the heat. Then to lunch with Blake at his rooms. Mr Sykes & — an old M.A. there. Talked some time afterwards & then to river & met Fletcher, who took us, rowed us round the backs. Landed long tennis match — between Johns & Peterhouse. Willie & Branscombe

seats. Haning the Dean asked us to tea but unfortunately we had another engagement. Went straight to Arthur Buss' rooms & had tea with him. Two friends there Hancock &—. Little A.B. made splendid host. All went walk afterwards. Willie to Hall. Met Branscombe at John's. Had splendid seats there, for service at end. I was next to the Vice Chancellor. Afterwards walked about John's, till Willie met us. Then walked all about backs & colleges. Branscombe took Mrs Buck home, Mabel & Maude went off to the Varsity Church, & Willie & I went round the backs again & then home. At 8.30 our "Musical Evening" began - Fletcher of Peterhouse & his brother with his violin - Pearce a tenor - Barton pianist. T . . . . tenor. Had some splendid music, Branscombe also sang. After they had gone had more music by ourselves. Then finished up with Evening Hymn & they took us home.

<u>Monday May 9th</u>

The Angelus woke me at 6.0. I got up & packed entirely before the rest got up. Breakfast at Willie's rooms. After breakfast went round Cambridge - then Willie had to go - so Mrs Buck took us round the colleges. Did Union previously. Then Peterhouse (7 chinned man) Pembroke - Corpus - St. Catherine's - King's - Queen's - Caius etc, So hot & tired. Home to ~~lunch at Branscombe's rooms~~. Afterwards had a little doze - being so tired with the heat. Then to lunch with Drake at his rooms. Mr Sykes & — (an old M.T.) there. Talked some time afterwards & then to river & met Fletcher, who took us, rowed us round the backs. Landed to see tennis match - between John's & Peterhouse. Willie & Hancock played. Then embarked again & up & down we went. Had many adventures & finally ended all things by Mater smashing an oar. That finished us we crestfallen — rowed home & kept the oar or rather blade as trophy. The patient & growing Fletcher took us to tea at the Union & great fun we had too. Retired dismally to pack after tea. Sadly oh so sadly & sent our luggage off to station with Mrs Buck & Maude. Mater, Willie & I walked & did not as I hoped, miss the train. oh. no. on those occasions the train is always distressingly late. 5 very mournful people bade adieu to each other at Cambridge Station & we went sadly off to London. At Liverpool St Walter Atward met Maude & Spencer & Posey met us. Got to West Ham at 10 p. & went to bed mournful three.

Cambridge. Second Edition

June 11th. To Cambridge by 9.40. Chaperoned an old lady of 73. Willie met me. Settled the old lady & then took hansom to 2 Quay Side. All the rest on river. They called for us & the "great" & we went en route for Grassey. Ade we landed had a jolly picnic — Turner & Arthur Bues with us. Had great fun. Embarked rowed a good way down the river. Then back in time to get good places at Ditton for the races. Waited there a long time & were frequently photographed. O. Bues Cox stamped. Got off well after races in good time, Thad most exciting times going home. Pursued 2 Johns men in a canoe. Saw 2 respectable old paterfamilias upset & drenched. Landed & back in tremendous haste to dress. Started walking by 9.15. to Peterhouse Ball. Splendidly arranged played. Then embarked again & up & down we went. Had many adventures & finally ended all things by Mabel smashing an oar. That finished us. We crestfallen - rowed home & kept the oar or rather blade as trophy. The patient & forgiving Fletcher took us to tea at the Union & great fun we had too. Retired dismally to pack after tea, sadly oh so sadly & sent our luggage off to station with M[rs] Buck & Maude. Mabel, Willie & I walked & did not as I hoped, miss the train. Oh no, on those occasions the train is always distressingly late. 5 very mournful people bade adieu to each other at Cambridge Station & 4 went sadly off to London. At Liver-pool St Walter Howard met Maude & Spencer & Percy met us. Got to West Ham at 10.0, & went to bed mournful & tired.

Cambridge, Second Edition

June 14th To Cambridge by 9.40. Chaperoned an old lady of 73, Willie met me. Settled the old lady & then took hansom to 2 Quay-Side. All the rest on river. They called for us & the "grub" & we went en route for Grassey. Here we landed, & had a jolly picnic - Turner & Arthur Buss with us. Had great fun. Embarked & rowed a good way down the river. Then back in time to get front places at Ditton for the races. Waited there a long time & were frequently photographed. A. Buss Cox & Trumper. Got off well after races in good time, & had most exciting times going home. Pursued 2 John's men in a canoe. Lost. Saw 2 respectable old paterfamiliases upset & drenched. Landed & back in tremendous haste to dress. Started walking in evening dress about 9.15 to Peterhouse Ball. Splendidly arranged.

Danced with Willie = Blake = Mallinson = Evans - Rush-
wood - Kimmins (Killens) = Potter + Johnson -
Enjoyed it immensely. Left about 3.30. The
dawn broke about 2.0 & the sun shone well.
All Cams men up, & out of windows -
Many in the road. Got to bed about 4.0.

June 15th. Wed.

Up again at 7.0. Mabel & I a walk before
breakfast. Shopping afterwards, & walk
round backs, & all about. Lunch with
Willie. To river in afternoon with books.
Stole B. & had tea. Boat procession. Chapel
at King's. Good seats. Procession afterwards.
Tea with G. Buss in his rooms - Hancox
Fox & Stilt there - Then home & dressed.
Mabel, G. Buss, Willie & I to Lee's Concert.
Very jolly. Grounds all lighted with
lanterns - Ices & promenade in interval.
Runaway horse afterwards - Walked home
round backs. Walk on quay. Bed - Killed

June 16th Thur.

Turner went down - Missed him at meals -
Early up. To printers before breakfast with
Willy for programmes. (On red brown. Called
on Norris at Christ's & met Roper there.)
G Buss to breakfast. All to tennis after.
Elliott & Bennett joined us. Quite a gymkhana
grounds. To Senate House to see degrees
given. Lunch. Did programmes after-
Then Chauns - they tried unsuccessfully
to slumber. Mrs. B. Willie & I to King's! Quite
Chapel. Shopping. Bought flowers! Tea at
the Union with Willie. Dressed for Willie's
ball at Barley's rooms. Walked there
by daylight about 8.0. So jolly - Dances.
Willie = Bennett = Allen = Roper = Pleys =
Evans = Norris - R Norris = Allen - Promenade
all round Creek - unorthodox proceeding.
Friday. Walk previous to breakfast. Unfortunately
to Varsity tennis ground etc. Breakfast
with G Buss - Hancock & Stilt there. Went
to Bell's rooms after for literature. Then to
Arthur's rooms for Stilt - Then to Robinson
Crusoe - Buss Stilt. Bennett & Buck.

Dances with Willie = Drake ≡ Mallinson ≣ Evans = Buss – Wood – Rimmens (Kittens) ≡ = Potter + Johnson. Enjoyed it immensely. Left about 3.30. The dawn broke about 2.0 & the sun shone well. All Caius men up, & out of windows - many in the road. Got to bed about 4.0.

June 15th Wed.

Up again at 7.0 Mabel & I a walk before breakfast. Shopping afterwards & walk round backs, & all about. Lunch with Willie. To river in afternoon with books. Stole p. & had bit. Boat procession. Chapel at King's. Good seats. Procession afterwards. Tea with A. Buss in his rooms. Hancox Fox & S . . . . there. Then home & dressed. Mabel, A. Buss, Willie & I to Lee's Concert. Very jolly. Grounds all lighted with lanterns & ices & promenade in interval. Runaway horse afterwards. Walked home & round backs. Waltz on quay. Bed - kittens.

June 16th Thurs.

Turner went down - missed him at meals. Early up. To printers before breakfast with Willie for programmes. (On Wed morn called on Norris at Christ's & met Roper there) A. Buss to breakfast. All to tennis after. S . . . . & Bennett joined us. Amalgamation grounds. To Senate House to see degrees given. Lunch. Did programmes after. Then changed - then tried ineffectually to slumber. Mrs B. Willie & I to Kings. Ante Chapel. Shopping. Bought flowers! Tea at the Union with Willie. Dressed for Willie's ball at Barley's rooms. Walked there by daylight about 8.0. So jolly. Dances Willie = Bennett = Allen = Roper = P . . . . = Evans = Norris – R. Norris = Valerie x Promenaded all round streets - unorthodox proceeding.

Friday. Walk previous to breakfast, unfortunately to Varsity tennis grounds etc. Breakfast with A. Buss - Hancock & S . . . . there. Went to S . . . .'s rooms après for literature. Then to Arthur's rooms for grub. Then to Robinson Crusoe. Buss S . . . . , Bennett & Buck

Willie & Bennett in canoe – rest of us in boat en route for lunching place. Rowed through numerous gates, down to lock. Got out & boat dragged up whilst we went. Put in two more miles & then stopped for lunch. Charming field – all forget me nots, may, marguerites etc. Walk after lunch. Then I being persuaded albeit trembling, got into canoe with Willie & off we went. Felt at once quite at home therein. Left rest far behind & went on & on & on till we finally reached Harston, 9 miles from Cambridge. Found a inlet & disembarked. Walked to village & in the Swan had shandygaff. Then explored village – admired Hall. & after waiting long time for those who came not, paddled our own canoe back to look for them. Found them far far away & Batie the champion Varsity swimming with them. Could not take. Finally triumphed & went to farm house at Haslingfield. Walked to village for bread. Then picnicked on bank. About 8.0 embarked in boat this time & commenced homeward journey. Got on finely. Darkness came on. Lovely evening. Reached Cambridge about 10.15. To A Burrs rooms & then to ours. Supper. Sadly packed & bed –

<u>Saturday June 18th</u>

Up early & packed. Others to Senate House W.P. Breakfast. Photo purchasing afterwards. About 11.0. Mabel, Willie & I in hansom to station – Caught 11.30 So sorry to leave. Changed at Bletchley. Rugby. Heat intense – No one but boys at home – Sad depression consequent on leaving fascinating Cambridge.

Willie & Bennett in Canoe - Rest of us in boat en route for lunching place. Rowed through human frogs, down to lock. Got out & boat dragged up to higher level. Put in two more miles & then stopped for lunch. Charming field - all forget me nots, may, marguerites etc etc. Walk after lunch. Then, I being persuaded albeit trembling, got into Canoe with Willie & off we went. Felt at once quite at home therein. Left rest far behind & went on & on & on till we finally reached Harston 9 miles from Cambridge. Found a mill & disembarked. Walked to village & in the Swan had Shandygaff. Then explored village - admired Hall & after waiting long time for those who came not, paddled our own canoe back to look for them. Found them far, far away & Batie the champion Varsity swimmer with them. Could <u>not</u> turn [?] Finally triumphed & went to farm house at Haslington [?Haslingfield].

Walked to village for bread. Then picnicked on bank. About 8.0 embarked in boat this time & commenced homeward journey. Got on finely. Darkness came on. Lovely evening. Reached Cambridge about 10.15. To A. Buss rooms & then to ours. Supper. Sadly packed & bed

<u>Saturday</u> June 18th

Up early & packed. Others to Senate House W. P. Breakfast. Photo purchasing afterwards. About 11.0. Mabel, Willie & I in hansom to station. Caught 11 . . . <u>so</u> sorry to leave. Changed at Bletchley & Rugby. Heat intense - No one but boys at home - sad depression consequent on leaving fascinating Cambridge.

London.

Tuesday. May 10th
Breakfast very late indeed – Mabel & I. Afterwards wrote many letters, an immense one to Mother. Worked after dinner. About 4.0 – Percy, Mabel, a small boy & I departed for Wanstead Park on top of an omnibus, no tram. Had long walk & eventually reached the lake. Chartered a boat & rowed about in mild imitation of the Cam. Had tea in boat. Walked afterwards all round the Park, & then back to tram & home. Wrote many letters before bed.
Wednesday. 11th
In morning Mrs. Buck, Mabel & I went shopping in Stratford. Did work. Then packed for Mysa. Left box at West Ham. Took various packages with me. Percy escorted me to Bow & to Chalk Farm, from whence I walked to Mysa. Maud had just arrived. After tea Maude & some girls went to the dinner of the Governesses Benevolent Institution at Willis Rooms – Earl Derby in Chair. Heard speeches & then home. Stole upstairs like mice as the house was wrapped in slumber.
Thursday. 12th
Maude & I set off by ourselves & went first to Ludovici collection of pupils works, & then took hansom to the Academy. Had lunch there & then home to dinner. In afternoon took hansom up to Hampstead & called on Mrs. Matheson. Saw Gladstone driving. In evening had drawing room all to ourselves. Wrote letters & read.
Friday. 13th
Maude & I off again. First to Water Colour which we much enjoyed. Then to Grosvenor which unfortunately we had

London

Tuesday May 10th

Breakfast very late indeed, Mabel & I. Afterwards wrote many letters, an immense one to Mother. Worked after dinner. About 4.0 Percy, Mabel, a small boy & I departed for Wanstead Park on top of an omnibus, no tram. Had long walk & eventually reached the lake. Chartered a boat & rowed about in mild imitation of the Cam. Had tea in boat. Walked afterwards all through the Park, & then back to tram & home. Wrote many letters before bed.

Wednesday 11th

In morning Mrs Buck, Mabel & I went shopping in Stratford. Did work. Then packed for Myra. Left box at West Ham & took various packages with me. Percy escorted me to Bow & to Chalk Farm from whence I walked to Myra. Maude had just arrived. After tea Maude & I & some girls went to the dinner of the Governesses Benevolent Institution at Willis Rooms - Earl Derby in Chair. Heard speeches & then home. Stole upstairs like mice as the house was wrapped in slumber.

Thursday 12th

Maude & I set off by ourselves & went first to Ludovici Collection of pupils works, & then took hansom to the Academy. Had lunch there & then home to dinner. In afternoon took hansom up to Hampstead & called on Mrs Mathieson. Saw Gladstone driving. In evening had drawing room all to ourselves. Wrote letters & read.

Friday 13th

Maude & I off again. First to Walter Colours which we much enjoyed. Then to Grosvenor which unfortunately we had rather rushing through. In afternoon letters drunk by ourselves. Miss Ru skirmished about. Finally Miss Fawcett, Maude & I went off to Evelyn Reeds & saw the Naturalist, which we much enjoyed.

Saturday 14th.

About 11.0 packed up & went off with Maude home to Oaklands. Cricklewood Lunch only Mrs Howard. Immediately after drove to Princes Hall Piccadilly a friend going also. Saw decorations for Queen to pass on her way to open Peoples' Palace. Recital by Harriette Kendall — very good indeed. Enjoyed it so much. Drove home again. Dinner 6.30. Mr Howard came home. Music afterwards. Made acquaintance of Walter Howard late in the evening.

Sunday 15th.

Walter, Maude & I to Church at Willesden walking — Mrs Howard in Brougham. We were late & had rather a crush for seats. Walked home again. Gladstone passed us, had splendid view. Dinner. After dinner Maude to Sunday school. Sat all afternoon in verandah talking to Walter till Maude came. Mr & Mrs Frandan came to tea. Talking. Garden etc till supper. They went. Read Zoroaster. Splendid book. Talked in drawing room till 11.3

Monday 16th. Finished Zoroaster & wrote letters. About 11.0 back to Myra Lodge. Little shopping in Chalk Farm & then wrote letters rather to hurry through. In afternoon letters & work by ourselves. Miss Buss skirmished about. Finally Miss Fawcett, Maude & I went off to German Reed's & saw the Naturalist, which we much enjoyed.

Saturday 14th

About 11.0 packed up & went off with Maude home to Oaklands, Cricklewood. Lunch, only Mrs Howard. Immediately after drove to Princes Hall Piccadilly, a friend going also. Saw decorations for Queen to pass on her way to open Peoples' Palace. Recital by Harriette Kendall - very good indeed Enjoyed it so much. Drove home again. Dinner 6.30. Mr Howard came home. Music afterwards. Made acquaintance of Walter Howard late in the evening.

Sunday 15th

Walter, Maude & I to Church at Willesden. We walked - Mrs Howard in brougham. We were late & had rather a crush for seats. Walked home again. Gladstone passed us, had splendid view. Dinner. After dinner Maude to Sunday School. Sat all afternoon in verandah talking to Walter, till Maude came. Mr & Mrs Frankau came. Tea. Talking. Garden etc till supper. They went. Read Zoraster. Splendid book. Talked in drawing room till 10.30

Monday 16th Finished Zoraster & wrote letters

About 11.0 back to Myra Lodge. Little shopping in Chalk Farm & then wrote letters

gll dinner. Letter from Willie. In consequence went down to West Ham in afternoon & stayed tea. Fetched some things. Percy started me back at night. Very late indeed. Reached Myra about 9.0. & was glad of supper.

Tuesday 17th. Wrote an immense number of letters in the morning. All lunch Miss Buss "at home" in afternoon. She had awful cold. Helped to entertain callers. One stayed tea. About 6.0 she, Miss Fawcett & I off to Lady Clancarty. Mr Mrs Kendal. Enjoyed it so. Came very tired when got home after, in fact dozed in a shaky omnibus!

Wednesday 18th. Letters & music all morning. Lunch sumptuous from Miss Paul – (greedy!) To post. After dinner called on Miss Brooks & stayed tea with her. Back about 6.30 – Nellie & I had drawing room alone. Letters & work. What a correspondent!

Thursday 19th. Again letters. Walked in rain down to school & did not enjoy the sight thereof or the walk. In afternoon Miss Fawcett & I to Islington after bonnets. Successful. Rain came on. I came home alone. Evening as usual.

Friday 20th. Shopping. Wet morning. Stayed in. Letters of course. Miss Buss went into Lincolnshire. Drawing room to myself. Society occasionally. Little walk to Ridleys with Miss Fawcett. Music with her afterwards.

till dinner. Letter from Willie. In consequence went down to West Ham in afternoon & stayed tea & fetched some things - Percy started me back at night. Very late indeed - Reached Myra about 9.0 & was glad of supper.

<u>Tuesday 17th</u> Wrote an immense number of letters in the morning, till lunch. Miss Buss "At Home" in afternoon - She had awful cold. Helped to entertain callers. One stayed tea - About 6.0 - she, Miss Fawcett & I off to Lady Clancarty - Mr & Mrs Kendal. Enjoyed it so much Very tired when got home after, in fact dozed in a shaky omnibus!

<u>Wednesday 18th</u> Letters & music all morning. Lunch sumptuous from Miss Paul - (greedy!) To post - After dinner called on Miss Brooks & stayed tea with her. Back about 6.30 - Nellie & I had drawing room alone. Letters & work. What a correspondent!

<u>Thursday 19th</u> Again letters. Walked in rain down to school & did not enjoy the sight thereof or the walk. In afternoon Miss Fawcett & I to Islington, after bonnets. Successful. Rain came on. I came home alone - Evening as usual.

<u>Friday 20th</u> Shopping. Wet morning - stayed in. Letters of course - Miss Buss went into Lincolnshire - Drawing Room to myself. Society occasionally. Little walk to Ridleys with Miss Fawcett - Music with her afterwards.

Saturday 21st. Town with Miss Fawcett. She home. Son to Whiteleys. Bagged candle home in 2 min. Late for lunch with girls to Concert at Princes Hall in afternoon. See programme. In evening down to West Ham.
Sunday 22nd. Awoke with an awful swelled face from cold! Wrapped it up in Sumptuous mantilla & said nothing. To Church. Mr. Buck not at home. Read "She" in afternoon. Again to Church. Percy took organist place & played splendidly. Letters
Monday 23rd. Had to get away because of face. About 10. o to Shadwell. Susie met me. In afternoon she, Lissie, Cousin & I off shopping in City & Regent St. Tea at Fatty's. Mr. Bray met us. We all went to theatre - Ruddygore. Enjoyed it so much. By Underground to Farringdon & Shadwell at Midnight.
Tuesday 24th. Early lunch. All of us off to Wild West. Enjoyed Buffalo Bill immensely. See programme & bills as advertisements say. In evening to the Musical Entertainment of the Mutual Improvement Society.
Wednesday 25th. Stayed in all morning. Susie & I off to Mrs. a after lunch. Then to Old Pupils Meeting. Not very many girls I knew. Walked home with Miss Buss. She came in, while Mrs. D. rattled [illegible] o[illegible] meal -

Saturday 21st Town with Miss Fawcett. She home. I on to Whiteleys - Dragged cauldron home in rain. Late for lunch. With girls to concert at Princes Hall in afternoon. See programme. In evening down to West Ham.
Sunday 22nd Awoke with an awful swelled face from cold! Wrapped it up in impromptu mantilla & said nothing. To Church. Mrs Buck not at home. Read "She" in afternoon - Again to Church. Percy took organists place & played splendidly. Letters.
Monday 23rd Glad to get away because of face. About 10.0 to Shadwell. Susie met me. In afternoon she, Sissie, cousin & I off shopping in City & Regent St. Tea at Gatty's. Mr Bray met us, we all went to theatre - Ruddigore. Enjoyed it so much. By underground to Farringdon St. Shadwell at midnight.
Tuesday 24th Early lunch. All of us off to Wild West. Enjoyed Buffalo Bill immensely. See programme on bills as advertisements say. In evening to the musical entertainment of the Mutual Improvement Society.
Wednesday 25th Stayed in all morning. Susie & I off to Myra after lunch. Then to Old Pupils Meeting. Not very many girls I knew. Walked home with Miss Buss. She came in, while Miss F . . . .

Thursday 26th – Susie & I to Bayswater & made final purchases – wedding present Annie etc. Had big packing up – after lunch Susie came to Euston with me & then left for Edgbaston & home. Devoured sweets & read Queen all the way. Jolly glad to see Calthorpe Road again – & thus ends London jokes & joys –

Comberford.

Tuesday. July 19th.

By 4·30 train to Tamworth. Alice met me, we picked up Annie & drove home, to Comberford – After tea, tennis for the others – Mr Blaxon for supper –

Wednesday. 20th. Odd doings & batterings morning. Practised Banjo assiduously. Drove to Wigginton. Anniversary of Uncle's death – Wreath on Slate. Saw Cemetery. Then drove to Windmill, & called on Tom Lawes. Tom & Emily & Flossie to tea – Tennis etc & Banjo.

Thursday 21st.

Drove Annie & Rhoda to Tamworth shopping in morning. In afternoon drove to Elford. Called on Mrs Cupunder & looked over Church. Most splendid place – drove on to the Coxons. Spent evening there. George drove over – walk down Ladywood Walk. Spent jolly musical evening after dark. Banjo much in request – in fact quite the feature of the evening, my poor little times much applauded!!!

Thursday 26th Susie & I to Bayswater & made final purchases. Wedding present Fannie etc. Had big packing up. After lunch Susie came to Euston with me & then hey for Edgbaston & home. Devoured sweets & read Queen all the way. So very glad to see Calthorpe Road again - & thus ends London jokes & joys

Comberford

Tuesday July 19th

By 4.30 train to Tamworth. Alice met me. We picked up Auntie & drove home to Comberford. After tea, tennis for the others. Mr Clarson for supper.

Wednesday 20th Odd doings & various - Morning. Practised Banjo assiduously. Drove to Wigginton. Anniversary of Uncle's death - Wreath on Grave. Saw Cemetery. Then drove to Windmill & called on Tom Lowes. Tom & Emily & Florrie to tea - Tennis etc & Banjo.

Thursday 21st

I drove Auntie & Rhoda to Tamworth shopping in morning. In afternoon drove to Elford. Called on Mrs Cripwell & looked over Church. Most splendid place. Drove on to the Coxons. Spent evening there. George drove over - Walk down Ladywood Walk. Spent jolly musical evening after dark. Banjo much in request - in fact quite the feature of the evening, my poor little tunes much applauded!!

Friday. 22nd - George & I farming in morning. Banjo practice. I drove round by Kettlebrook & Tamworth to Dosthill & Mount Side in afternoon. Annie with me. Tea with Cheatles. Back & much consternation when Mitchell Cony fetch Alice to Astley. She went! Lizzie & Charlie over from Whateley, to supper. Also Frances Parsons -

Saturday 23rd. Again farming. Repair ravages of naughty bunnies! To Wiggington to take wreath in afternoon - I drove. Annie & Rhoda. Then round to Windmill to tennis party. Annie drove home. Rhoda & I stayed. Mr Barningham there. A Nameless Croesus! Also Mr Shaw came etc. Tennis. I danced. After supper - Music banjo & Handel. George, I & Rhoda walked home & arrived weary. Peregrinated through village & saluted the Clarsons with National Anthem -

Sunday. 24th. I drove Annie to church & home again. Rain came on. Mr Barningham came appeared in storm. Walked in village & then Mr Shaw appeared too - Walk then it rained hard. Tea - After music & confab. Sat in porch. Tom & Emily came & little Florrie - Supper. Great fun! never laughed so much before, & Sunday too!

Friday 22nd George & I farming in morning. Banjo practice. I drove round by Kettlebrook & Tamworth to Dosthill & Mount Side in afternoon, Auntie with me. Tea with Cheatles. Back and much consternation to find Mitchell come to fetch Alice to Ashby. She went! Lizzie & Charlie over from Whateley, to supper. Also Frances Parsons.

Saturday 23rd Again farming. Repaired ravages of naughty bunnies! To Wiggington to take wreath in afternoon - I drove Auntie & Rhoda. Then round to Windmill to tennis party. Auntie drove home. Rhoda & I stayed. Mr Barmingham there, a brainless Croesus! Also Mr Shaw came etc. Tennis. I banjoed. After supper - music banjo & cards etc. George, I & Rhoda walked home, & arrived weary. Peregrinated through village & saluted the Carsons with National Anthem -

Sunday 24th I drove Auntie to church & home again. Rain came on. Mr Barmingham appeared in storm! Walked in village & then Mr Shaw appeared too - Walk then it rained hard. Tea. After music & confabs. Sat in porch. Tom & Emily came & little Florrie. Supper. Great fun! Never laughed so much before, & Sunday too!

Monday 25th. Farming & inspected stables with George. Annie & I trotted all about everywhere. Pack after dinner to entertainment of Swimming at the Baths. Tea at the Windmill. Then George drove me to the Station & started me off by 6.20 for Home Sweet Home.

Langley Priory.

Saturday. July 30th.
Mother started me off by 12.15. train. Station very full & train very late. Travelled with Evans. Changed at Derby & reached Tonge about 3.0. Hanford met me with the Pony Carriage. All at Home to meet me. After tea. Explored gardens & after supper walked in grounds till bed time.

Sunday. 31st.
Thunder & rain early. Then cleared off. All of us to church at Diseworth. I drove with Mrs Shakespear & Connie, the rest walked. Called at Vicarage afterwards. After dinner read etc till tea time. After tea Gertie & I walked to Breedon to church, but the rain & thunder came on & frightened us, so we came home & walked about till supper & then read in drawing room.

Monday 1st. Gardens, all of us after breakfast. Gertie & I walked to Diseworth & called at the Vicarage. After dinner had a Tennis party at Langley Priory. Of course worked on. Tea in garden under the Cedar. All left about 7.0. The

Monday 25th Farming & inspected stables with George. Auntie & I trotted all about everywhere. Packed. After dinner to entertainment of swimming at the Baths. Tea at the Windmill. Then George drove me to the station & started me off by 6.20 for Home Sweet Home.

Langley Priory

Saturday July 30th
Mother started me off by 12.15 train. Station very full & train very late. Travelled with Evans. Changed at Derby & reached Tonge about 2.0. Hanford met me with the pony carriage. All at home to meet me. After tea - explored gardens & after supper walked in grounds till bed time.

Sunday 31st
Thunder & rain early. Then cleared off. All of us to church at Diseworth. I drove with Mrs Shakespear & Connie, the rest walked. Called at vicarage afterwards. After dinner read etc, till tea time. After tea Gertie & I walked to Breedon to church but the rain & thunder came on & frightened us, so we came home & walked about till supper & then had music in drawing room.

Monday 1st Gardens, all of us after breakfast. Gertie & I walked to Diseworth & called at the vicarage. After dinner had a tennis party at Langley Priory, I of course looked on. Tea in gardens under the cedar. All left about 7.0. The

br'ear wife & mother stayed to supper
walk round till 10.0.
Tuesday 2nd. Gardens as usual for
fruit. Worked & dressed dolls in
Schoolroom. Mrs. S. Connie Ina & I
drove in the waggonette about 4.0. to
the Vanes at Melbourne Hall to a
tennis party. Lovely. gardens, a
copy of those at Versailles. Yew
avenue & tunnel. Went over lovely
old Norman Church. In the
morning, went a walk round,
Ina, Gertie & I by the way. Drove
home through Melbourne about
7.30. After supper, up & down the
terrace in the moonlight.
Wednesday 3rd.
Ina. Gertie & I to Diseworth in morning
Called at the one shop & went
also in the Churchyard. Read in
the hammock till dinner time.
After dinner Connie, Gertie, Charlie
& I drove in waggonette to the Trent
at Kings Newton. Met the Briggs en
famille with ammunition for tea.
Rowed in Canoe & boat down to Boat
house at Castle Donnington. Had tea
Boiled kettle. Scrambled up to park,
and Donnington's afterwards. Connie
& I walked home to Kings Newton
with Mr Briggs. Met Carriage & drove
home. After supper. Went a walk
along the terrace.

Vicar, wife & brother stayed to supper. Walk round till 10.0.

Tuesday 2nd Gardens as usual, for fruit. Worked & dressed dolls in schoolroom. Mrs S, Connie, Ina & I drove in the waggonette about 4.0 to the Fanes at Melbourne Hall to a tennis party. Lovely. Gardens a copy of those at Versailles. Yew avenue or tunnel. Went over lovely old Norman Church. In the morning, went a walk round, Ina, Gertie & I by the way. Drove home through Melbourne about 7.30. After supper, up & down the terrace in the moonlight.

Wednesday 3rd

Ina, Gertie & I to Diseworth in morning. Called at the one shop & went also in the churchyard. Read in the hammock till dinner time. After dinner Connie, Gertie, Charlie & I drove in waggonette to the Trent at Kings Newton. Met the Briggs en famille with ammunition for tea. Rowed in Canoe & boat down to Boat house at Castle Donnington - Had tea. Boiled kettle. Scrambled up to park, Lord Donnington's afterwards. Connie & I walked home to Kings Newton with Mr Briggs. Met carriage & drove home. After supper, went a walk along the terrace

Thursday 4th. Gardens & walk dun
having previously dressed each
one doll under the Cedar tree
After lunch drove to Ashbourne to
School treat in Vicar's garden
Had great fun. Band. Danc
& played the whole evening till
8.15 then drove home. & walk
all evening till 10.0.
Friday 5th. Gardens, & rowed
Gertie on the lake for about
an hour. Then Ida, Gertie
& went a walk. After dinner
packed up my things & got
ready for starting at 4.0.
Changed at Derby. & found an
escort, & got home much late
owing to the strike of the Midland
men. Stuart met me.

<u>Thursday 4th</u> Gardens & walk round, having previously dressed each our doll under the cedar tree. After lunch drove to Diseworth to school treat in Vicar's garden - had great fun. Band. Danced & played the whole evening till 8.15, then drove home. Walk all round till 10.0.

<u>Friday 5th</u> Gardens, & rowed Gertie on the lake for about an hour. Then Ina, Gertie & I went a walk. After dinner packed up my things & got ready for starting at 4.0. Changed at Derby, & found an escort, & got home much late owing to the strike of the Midland men. Stuart met me.

Scotland.

Aug.
8. Birmingham – Glasgow. Central Station.
9. Glasgow – Greenock. (Train.
Greenock – Ardrishaig – "Columba".
Ardrishaig – Crinan – " "Linnet".
Crinan – Oban – " "Chevalier". 90
10. Oban – Ballachulish "Mountaineer
Ballachulish – Glencoe – (Coach) back 10
11. Oban – Staffa & Iona – "Pioneer".
12. Oban – Ford (Coach. 29 miles
Ford – Loch Awe "Countess Breadalbane
Loch Awe – Oban (Train. 16 38.
13. Oban – Gairloch " "Glencoe". 40
14. Gairloch – Poolewe (Walk. 12.
15. Gairloch – Achnasheen (Coach. 28.
Achnasheen – Inverness (Train.
16. Inverness – Co pach " "Glengarry". 62
Co pach – Fort William " "Gondolier".
17. Fort William – Kingussie. (Coach. 50½
Kingussie – Pitlochry – (Train.
Pitlochry – Dunkeld – (Train.
18. Dunkeld – Braemar – (Train. 13
19. Braemar – (Coach. 48.
20. Braemar Coromulzie Falls. (Walk.
Braemar. – Ballater – Coach. 18.
Ballater – Aberdeen – (Train. 43½
Aberdeen – Perth (
Perth – Dunkeld – (" 153+
21. Dunkeld – Falls of Bran (Walk. 6.
22. Dunkeld Trossachs
(Aberfeldy 6 Kenmore 15 Killin 17 Callender.)
23. Trossachs 1½ Loch Katrine
Stronachlacken – Inversnaid – Balloch.
Glasgow – Edinburgh –
24. Edinburgh – Birmingham.

Scotland.

Coupar Angus.

Forfar.

Edinburgh.

Devil's Elbow.

Aberdeen.

Perth.

Crinan Canal.

Inverlochy Castle.

Aberfeldy.

Oban.

Ballater.

Ballahulish.

Loch Lomond.

Pass of Glencoe.

Spital of Glenshee.

Inversnaid.

Tarbet.

Three Sisters.

New Mar Lodge.

Glen Beg.

R. Cluny.

Old Mar Castle.

Staffa.

Iona.

Abergeldie.

R. Dee.

Strathpeffer.

Tobermory.

Balloch.

Mull.

Luss.

Glen Orchary.

Braemar.

Castle Urquhart.

Crinan.

Kingussie.

Scotland.

Inverauld Arms - Lion's Face Rock - Cluny Castle.

Loch Maree.

Beauly. Loch Earn. Ford. Callender. Portree - Invergarry Castle.

Glasgow. Pass of Brander. Loch Laggan. Invergarry Castle.

Fife Arms - Killiecrankie - Loch Lolly -

Balmoral. Killin Junction. Paisley. Falls of Bran. Loch Arracher.

Mar Castle. Loch Awe. Trossachs.

Pass of Leny. Scone Palace -

Fort William.

Kinlochewe - Pass of Melford - Ardconnell Castle -

Scott Monument. Lorne - Shonachlachan. Oban - Old Mar Lodge

Gairloch - Corpach -

Braemar - Loch Katrine -

Inverary - Edinburgh Castle.

Toolewe - Coronation -

Loch Tay. Dumbarton Castle. Silver Strand. Falls. Rothsay.

Killin. Greenock - Falls of Foyers.

Dunoon - Inchnaskeen. Howerdale -

Ben Alder deer forest - Ellen's Isle - Moy -

Scotland.

August 8th Monday.
Papa, Mother & I started from New Stre
by 8.50 train. Stuart started us. Chang
at Carlisle reached Glasgow at 6.
First part of journey hot – then dull
& a little rain. Trains very full lo
of people travelling about. Had
successive pretty babies & small
girls to gaze at in our carriages.
One party had a little stove & all
complete & had a little cooking
performance on its own account –
much to Papa's disgust. I slumbered

Scotland

August 8th Monday

Papa, Mother & I started from New Street by 8.50 train. Stuart started us. Changed at Carlisle & reached Glasgow at 6.20. First part of journey hot - then dull & a little rain. Trains very full, lots of people travelling about. Had successive pretty babies & small girls to gaze at in our carriages. One party had a little stove & all complete & had a little cooking performance on her own account - much to Papa's disgust. I slumbered

twice en route. Central Hotel Glasgow.
Had our meal about 6.45, & a
telegram of welcome to Auld Reekie
arrived. Mother rather knocked up.
so Papa & I went out alone down
Glasgow by moonlight & gaslight &
electric light. St George's Square —
Municipal Buildings — & splendid
Post Office. Many, in fact nearly
all shops closed. Joined Mother
in drawing room & then to bed
moderately early in preparation
for the morrow.

Tuesday. Aug. 9th.

Up & breakfasted early. Train 8.5 to Greenock,
to save unpleasant smells of steamer down
Clyde. Dumbarton Castle. Joined Columba
at Greenock & went away down to Ardrishaig
passing Rothsay & many other calling
places down the Clyde. Walked a short
way from Columba to Linnet on the
Crinan Canal. Luggage went overland.
Passed through 9 locks. Got in course
of time to Crinan & there got on board
the Chevalier for Oban. Very windy &
wet passage. Got jolly places at bow
of boat well sheltered. Lunched on
board Columba. Grand scramble to
find luggage. At Oban went to Great
Western Hotel. Before dinner Papa &
I went to Alexandra — Station. Caledonian
to find if possible Mr Kirkwood. He had
not come. Table d'hôte 7.0. Afterwards
Papa & I out again — to pier to see
steamer come in & to Grand Hotel.

twice en route. Central Hotel Glasgow
Had our meal about 6.45, & a
telegram of welcome to Auld Reekie
arrived. Mother rather knocked up
so Papa & I went out alone & viewed
Glasgow by moonlight & gaslight &
electric light. St George's Square -
Municipal Buildings - & splendid
Post Office. Many, in fact nearly
all shops closed. Joined Mother
in drawing room & then to bed
moderately early in preparation
for the morrow.

Tuesday. Aug. 9th

Up and breakfasted early. Train 8.5 to Greenock
to save unpleasant smells of steamer down
Clyde. Dumbarton Castle. Joined Columba
at Greenock & went away down to Ardrishaig,
passing Rothesay and many other calling
places down the Clyde. Walked a short
way from Columba to Linnet on the
Crinan Canal. Luggage went overland.
Passed through 9 locks. Got in course
of time to Crinan & there got on board
the Chevalier for Oban. Very windy &
wet passage - got jolly places at bow
of boat well sheltered. Lunched on
board Columba. Grand skirmish to
find luggage. At Oban went to Great
Western Hotel - before dinner Papa &
I went to Alexandra - Station - Caledonian
to find if possible Mr. Kirkwood. He had
not come. Table d'hôte 7.0. Afterwards
Papa & I out again - to pier to see
steamer come in & to Grand with

no better success in finding Mr Kirkwood
I felt embarrassed & very sleepy, so about
9.0. Came in & retired! G.W.Co-

Wednesday. Aug 10th. Slept till 8.0! Break
fast at 9.0. Afterwards explored Oban &
did small amount of shopping - Gloves
4¾ etc! Sat on Promenade - & sketched
or attempted to do so. Took steamer
"Mountaineer" at 12.45 down to
Ballachulish - Splendid day, lovely
sail. Enjoyed it so very much. Everything
seemed to make the pictures. Lunched
on board. At Ballachulish took coach
for Glencoe. Had box seat & a very
jolly Scotch girl with me. Terrible
Episode of N.M.C. Clergyman & his bag,
& how it was lost & found again.
Had 5 good horses & a capital driver,
& we did go to the Pass of Glencoe.
They simply flew up & down the hills,
urged on by whistles, whoops & shouts
which made it most exciting - from the
driver. Pass of Glencoe splendid - Caught
steamer back at Ballachulish at 6.30
Tea on board. Papa found 2 very nice
men friends from London, & Mother two
Stewarts from Watford. I had very good
time, all things included & sat some
time under shadow of boat, on the side
watching N.M.C's & sea gulls. Reached
Oban about 8.30 - Straight to Great
Western. Mr. Kirkwood & Mr. Ward came
to call. Meal - then Papa & I went on
the promenade & met Mr. Kirkwood
Promenaded - Called at Station Hotel
then they came back to our Hotel &
sat talking in drawing room - then left them

no better success in finding M[r] Kirkwood. I felt sunburnt & very sleepy, so about 9.0 came in & retired! N.M.C.s -

Wednesday. Aug 10th Slept till 8.0! Breakfast at 9.0. Afterwards explored Oban & did small amount of shopping - gloves 7¾ etc! Sat on Promenade - I sketched or attempted to do so. Took steamer "Mountaineer" at 12.45 down to Ballachulish - splendid day & lovely sail. Enjoyed it so very much. Everything seemed to make a picture. Lunched on board. At Ballachulish took coach for Glencoe. Had Box Seat & a very jolly Scotch girl with me. Terrible episode of N.M.C. clergyman & his bag & how it was lost and found again. Had 5 good horses & a capital driver, & we did go to the Pass of Glencoe. They simply flew up & down the hills, urged on by whistles, whoops & shouts - which made it most exciting - from the driver. Pass of Glencoe splendid - Caught steamer back at Ballachulish at 6.30 Tea on board. Papa found 2 very nice men friends from London, & Mother two Stewarts from Watford. I had very good time, all things included & sat some time under shadow of boat, on the side, watching N.M.Cs & seagulls. Reached Oban about 8.30 - straight to Great Western. M[r] Kirkwood and M[r] Ward came to call. Meal. Then Papa and I went on the promenade & met M[r] Kirkwood. Promenaded - called at Station Hotel. Then they came back to our Hotel, & sat talking in drawing room - then I left them.

Met Mr & Mrs Pearson – 2 dements –
Thursday. August 11th
Up Early. Breakfast 7.15. On steamer at 8.–
for Staffa & Iona. Mr Kirkwood Mr Osborne–
Mr Ward with us. Blowy & cold & dull at
first. Got to Iona. an hour allowed &
I went on shore & with a party explored
old Cathedral & old Church of St Colum
Bought shells, sea urchin & stones
Noisy small boys. Touched on board
to Staffa – another hours rest. To
Island in little boats to see Fingal
Cave. Splendid. Colours grand. Climb
all inside & up to top of outside.
73 in one boat! Terrible swell on
soon after we started. Steamer–Green
rolled horribly–many ill. Indian
Prince on board. Views & colours of
mountains & distances lovely.
Sun came out & altered & transformed
everything. Had splendid homeward
journey. Clergyman bores. Home to
Oban about 6.15. Dinner 7.0. Out
afterwards to get some elder flower
water for my sunburnt visage–
Joined Messrs Kirkwood – Ward – Osborne
a walk past end of promenade.
Sat on Hotel balcony. Band played in
front. Awfully sleepy. Afterwards in
drawing room for short time. Wrote
letters before dinner –
Friday. 12th
Took it "out" till 8.0 o'clock. Breakfasted
at 9.0 – Started from door of hotel by
coach at 9.40. Said farewell to 3 friends

Met M^{r} & Mrs Pierson - 2 Demuths
Thursday. August 11th
Up early. Breakfast 7.15. On steamer at 8.0 for Staffa & Iona. Mr Kirkwood Mr Osborne - M^{r}. Ward with us. Blowy & cold & dull at first. Got to Iona - an hour allowed us I went on shore & with a party explored old Cathedral & old Church of St. Columba. Bought shells, sea urchin & stones from small boys. Lunched on board. To Staffa - another hour's rest. To island in little boats to see Fingals Cave. Splendid. Colours grand. Climbed all inside & up to top of outside. 7 [?] in one boat! Terrible swell on soon after we started. Steamer - Grenadier rolled horribly - many ill. Indian prince on board. Views & colours of mountains & distances lovely. Sun came out & altered & transformed everything. Had splendid homeward journey. Clergyman & sons. Home to Oban about 6.15. Dinner 7.0. Out afterwards to get some elder flower water for my sunburnt visage. Joined Messrs Kirkwood - Ward - Osborne. A walk past end of promenade. Sat on Hotel balcony. Band played in front. Awfully sleepy. Afterwards in drawing room for short time. Wrote letters before dinner.
Friday 12th
"Took it out" till 8.0 o'clock. Breakfasted at 9.0 - Started from door of hotel by coach at 9.40. Said farewell to 3 friends

at Station Hotel en passant. Drove 32
miles through lovely mountain scenery.
Pass of Melford to the village of Ford,
where we got down & found the steamer
"Countess of Breadalbane" waiting us.
Steamed right across Loch Awe calling
at 2 piers to town of "Loch Awe".
Papa & I went to Hotel there. Nice people
& "Mr Kemp" on coach & steamer. Terrible
showers occasionally. Waited 1/4 hour
then train came up & we went off
to Oban, through pretty country or
rather pretty is not the right word,
it should be grand. Just in time
for table d'hote. Met the Cokes of Norwood
again! Papa & I went out to buy
photos. Long promenade. Then in
to peck after short time in
drawing room. Many friends new &
old seemed to turn up. It was quite
sad to think this was our last
evening in Oban. much as I had
hated it at first.

Saturday. 13th.

Started very early. Steamer "Glencoe" left
Oban at 7.0 so we breakfasted on board.
Very sorry indeed to leave. Sea deceptive,
looked like a mill pond in Oban bay, but
outside there was "good deal of swell on
while we breakfasted, insomuch that
I felt rather relieved when breakfast
was over. Called at many places, as
far as Tobermory the same as our
return from Staffa. Many ferry boats
came out. Had a most glorious day
rain at times but not enough to trouble

at Station Hotel en passant. Drove 32 miles through lovely mountain scenery. Pass of Melford to the village of Ford, where we got down & found the steamer - Countess of Breadalbane waiting us - steamed right across Loch Awe, calling at 2 piers to town of Loch Awe [Lochawe]. Papa & I went to hotel there. Nice people & Mr Kemp on coach & steamer. Terrible showers occasionally. Waited ¼ hour then train came up, & we went off to Oban, through pretty country, or rather pretty is not the right word, it should be grand. Just in time for table d'hôte. Met the Cokes of Norwich again! Papa & I went out to buy photos, & on promenade - Then in to pack after short time in reading room. Many friends new & old seemed to turn up - it was quite sad to think this was our last evening in Oban - much as I had hated it at first -

Saturday 13th

Started very early. Steamer "Glencoe" left Oban at 7.0 - so we breakfasted on board Very sorry indeed to leave. Sea deceptive looked like a mill pond in Oban bay, but outside there was a good deal of swell on while we breakfasted, insomuch that I felt rather relieved when breakfast was over. Called at many places, as far as Tobermory the same as our return from Staffa. Many ferry boats came out. Had a most glorious day - rain at times but not enough to trouble us.

Lunched on board & tea also. I wrote long letter which the steward took ashore at Salen — & then sketched a rather tried to sketch anyone or anything in the least degree inter took much interest in everyone on board & found out about them. The Captain a charming man & so kind. Muirs. Burrells. & many oth who became friends eventually. Day seemed to fly. Stormy & wet weather drov everyone down. After calling at Port very rough indeed — Greens of Becken came on board there. Reached Gairloc about 7.30 & drove straight to hotel. Supp walk & looked round. In drawing room short time, then saw Northern Light then felt too sleepy to stop up any long

Sunday. 14th.

Breakfast at 9.30! Terribly late. Did not get up till 8.0! Little walk with Papa get an appetite. After breakfast St off & walked to Poolewe 6 miles off. Scotch mist falling the greater part the time. Sat under a rock during worst shower. Passed 2 gipsy encamp & one tourist tent — talked to everyone we met, including the undecided newly married couple. The Burrells — father son caught us up, as we got into Poo went to the small hotel & had some lun Just encountered all the church goers co out of kirk. Many Highlanders in kilts full Highland dress. After short time set off back again. The two parents &

Lunched on board & tea also. I wrote a long letter which the steward took ashore at Salen - & then sketched or rather tried to sketch anyone or anything in the least degree interesting. Took much interest in everyone on board & found out about them. The Captain a charming man & so kind - Muirs - Burrells - & many others, who became friends eventually. Day seemed to fly. Stormy & wet weather drove everyone down. After calling at Portree very rough indeed - Greens of Beckenham came on board there. Reached Gairloch about 7.30 & drove straight to hotel. Supper, walk & looked round. In drawing room a short time, then saw Northern Lights, & then felt too sleepy to stop up any longer.

Sunday 14th

Breakfast at 9.30! Terribly late. Did not get up till 8.0! Little walk with Papa to get an appetite. After breakfast started off & walked to Poolewe 6 miles off. Scotch mists falling the greater part of the time. Sat under a rock during the worst shower. Passed 2 gypsy encampments & one tourist tent - Talked to everyone we met, including the undecided newly married couple. The Burrells - father & son caught us up, as we got into Poolewe. Went to the small hotel & had some milk. Just encountered all the church goers coming out of kirk. Many Highlanders in kilts & full Highland dress. After short time set off back again, the two parents together, the two children together - The Children outwalked the parents who sat down to rest - & in spite of waitings reached the Hotel considerably sooner & encountered a second lot of people from another Kirk - 3.30 - Dressed for dinner - at 6.0. Jolly - but the Chadwicks made themselves conspicuous & obnoxious - Afterwards Papa & I walked to Flowerdale - & away up to their waterfall. Met Mr & Mrs Green on the way & had a long talk with them - Such nice people. In spite of mud reached top of the glen & then rushed home, slowly in gathering darkness. Just late for tea, so had it by ourselves in deserted room. Drawing room for short time -

Monday. 15th.

Breakfast at about 8.0 - Jolly as usual. Packed afterwards. Then came down & had time for just short adieus etc. Got box seat for myself - lucky as usual. Mrs & Dr Cains the other box seat - a charming woman. Somehow have met such very nice people the whole way. So very sorry to leave Gairloch - feel so much at home there. Drove with 2 changes of horses right away to Auchnasheen by Loch Maree 29 miles. Coach crowded with passengers & luggage. The Glen of Docharty was lovely. Rain fell several times - & it was awfully cold by the time we got to Auchnasheen station. Most people

& the two children together - The children outwalked the parents who sat down to rest - & in spite of waitings reached the Hotel considerably sooner & encountered a second lot of people from another Kirk - 3.30 - Dressed for dinner - at 5.0 Jolly - but the Chadwicks made themselves conspicuous & obnoxious - Afterwards Papa & I walked to Flowerdale - & away up to their waterfall. Met M^r & Mrs Green on the way & had a long talk with them - such nice people. In spite of mud reached top of the glen & then rushed home, owing to gathering darkness. Just late for tea, so had it by ourselves in deserted room. Drawing room for short time.

Monday 15th

Breakfast at about 8.0. Jolly as usual. Packed afterwards. Then came down & had time for just short adieus etc. Got box seat for myself - lucky as usual. M^rs & Dr Cams the other box seat - a charming woman. Somehow have met such very nice people the whole way. So very sorry to leave Gairloch - felt so much at home there. Drove with 2 changes of horses right away to Auchnasheen by Loch Maree - 29 miles. Coach crowded with passengers & luggage. The Glen of Docharty was lovely, rain fell several times - & it was awfully cold by the time we got to Auchnasheen station. Most people had dinner – we just very light refreshment. Train of course – being Highland Railway – late. Started about 4.10 & reached Inverness about 7.0 – not so bad, considering that the train is liable to be stopped by anyone, anywhere. Went straight to Caledonian Hotel. Found a little heap of letters. Dinner 7.30. Afterwards Papa & I went out for a stroll. Saw Suspension Bridge, Castle, & Cathedral, as well as the gloom & rain would allow us. When tired of rain & damp came in. After being in drawing room some time writing up diary – retired. (I was tremendously hungry by dinner.) Sat by a charming little man, or rather he sat by me – evidently a little old bachelor. A most amusing little man.

Tuesday. 16th.

Up early – oh how early we are getting. Called at 5.30 & just a cup of coffee before starting for the boat at 6.30. An omnibus full. The "Glengarry" left the Muirtown pier at 7.0 sharp – & we did not breakfast till 8.30. Sat as usual on top deck for a long time, then afterwards got sketch book & chair & sat in end of boat & tried to sketch some of the people – much to the horror of a lady's maid who thought I was doing her, & absolutely fled! At Foyers Falls disembarked & walked hard to the Falls getting there before the vehicles.

had dinner. We just very light refreshment. Train of course - being Highland Railway - late. Started about 4.10 & reached Inverness about 7.0 - not so bad, considering that the train is liable to be stopped by anyone, anywhere. Went straight to Caledonian Hotel, & found a little heap of letters. Dinner 7.30. Afterwards Papa and I went out for a stroll. Saw Suspension Bridge, Castle & Cathedral as well as the gloom & rain would allow us. When tired of rain & damp came in, & after being in drawing room some time & writing up diary - retired. I was tremendously hungry by dinner & sat by a charming little man, or rather he sat by me - evidently a little old bachelor, a most amusing little man.

Tuesday 16th

Up early - oh how early we are getting. Called at 5.30 & just a cup of coffee before starting for the boat at 6.30. An omnibus full. The "Glengarry" left the Muirtown Pier at 7.0 sharp - & we did not breakfast till 8.30. Sat as usual on top deck for a long time, then afterwards got sketch book and diary & sat in end of boat & tried to sketch some of the people - much to the horror of a lady's maid, who thought I was doing her, & absolutely fled! At Foyer's Falls disembarked & walked hard to the Falls getting there before the vehicles &

before Papa - They would have been splendid had there been more water, as it was they were very beautiful. Got back to steamer almost first. Again at Fort Augustus got off boat, while it went through the locks, & inspected the shops - Had some milk from an old woman who was most amusing. Went on sketching at odd times when no one watched & nothing much happened on board till we got to Banavie. The Caledonian Canal was very lovely in its natural parts. At Banavie all changed from the "Glengarry" & had to wait an immense time for the "Mountaineer" which was very late. The "good looking purser with the romantic history" was on board. The sun was scorching hot, more so than ever before. We crossed over to Fort William & got off the boat, & said good-bye to the old friends. Went to the "Caledonian" & at first thought it an awful place, but opinion changed afterwards. The nice Scotch & the 2 mothers came also. Dinner about 4.30 - ourselves & one young man - Scotch, who made himself both agreeable & amusing. All to drawing room afterwards - Papa & I went down to the pier, but as the boat was so late, continually came away without seeing it. Drawing room again. Made out our plans & route. Mother not very well. To bed about 9.30 - in preparation for the morrow.

Wednesday. 14th.

Still earlier! Awoke at 4.45! & called the others.

before Papa. They would have been splendid had there been more water, as it was they were very beautiful. Got back to steamer almost first. Again at Fort Augustus got off boat, while it went through the locks, and inspected the shops - Had some milk from an old woman who was most amusing. Went on sketching at odd times when no one watched & nothing much happened on board till we got to Banavie. The Caledonian Canal was very lovely in its natural parts. At Banavie all changed from the "Glengarry" & had to wait an immense time for the "Mountaineer" which was very late. The "good looking purser with the romantic history" was on board. The sun was scorching hot, more so than ever before. We crossed over to Fort William and got off the boat, and said Good-bye to the old friends. Went to the "Caledonian" & at first thought it an awful place, but opinions changed afterwards. The nice sister & the 2 brothers came also. Dinner about 7.30 - ourselves & one young man - Scotch, who made himself both agre-able & amusing. All to drawing room afterwards - Papa & I went down to the pier, but as the boat was so late, eventually came away without seeing it. Drawing room again. Made out our plans & route. Mother not very well. To bed about 9.30 - in prepar-ation for the morrow.

Wednesday 17th

Still earlier! I woke at 4.45! & called the others

at 5.40 we breakfasted & at 6.0 started on the Coach from the hotel door. A delightful 4 in hand, & an old stage coach — the mail coach — & Papa & I had the best places. Mother not being well, went inside unfortunately. From Fort William to Kingussie was 50 miles & we did it by 12.20 — with 4 stages. Stopped at Moy for breakfast — 10 minutes allowed. An old historical farmhouse, very comfortable indeed. Two fishermen, Londoners from the Alexandra, had the box seat. At Moy another fisherman — amateur — got up on our seat & turned out an awfully nice man & eventually travelled all the way to Pitlochry with us on his way to Edinburgh. The journey by coach was only too short. After getting down at Pullars at Kingussie we got all our luggage settled & went to the station. During the way along the coach kept picking up the mail bags, passengers, & parcels posts till we were piled up to the very top, & going down the last hills, I had a bad time of it as the hampers being heavy would slip on to my back. From Kingussie to Pitlochry by train getting there about 3.20. As the hotel would have kept us rooms out (Fisher's Hotel) we simply lunched there & went on by 5.0 train to Fisher's Royal Hotel Dunkeld. The rain prevented us going round place. Again rain — at Dunkeld — dinner at 7.0. I wanted to see the Cathedral, but it again rained. Wrote in drawing room, diary & letters.

At 5.40 we breakfasted & at 6.0 started on the Coach from the hotel door. A delightful 4 in hand & an old stage coach - the Mail Coach - & Papa & I had the best places. Mother not being well, went inside unfortunately. From Fort William to Kingussie was 50 miles & we did it by 12.20 - with 4 stages. Stopped at Moy for breakfast - 10 minutes allowed. An old historical farmhouse very comfortable indeed. Two fishermen, Londoners from the Alexandra, had the box seat. At Moy another fisherman - amateur - got up on our seat & turned out an awfully nice man & eventually travelled all the way to Pitlochry with us on his way to Edinburgh. The journey by Coach was only too short. After getting down at Pullars at Kingussie we got all our luggage settled & went to the station. During the way along the coach kept picking up the mail bags, passengers, & parcels posts till we were piled up to the very top, & going down the last hills, I had a bad time of it as the hampers being heavy would slip on to my back. From Kingussie to Pitlochry by train, getting there about 3.20. As the hotel would have to get us rooms out (Fisher's Hotel) we simply lunched there & went on by 5.0 train to Fisher's Royal Hotel Dunkeld. The rain prevented us going round place. Again rain - at Dunkeld - dinner at 7.0. I wanted to see the Cathedral, but it again rained. Wrote in drawing room, diary & letters.

Thursday. 18th.
Had a treat & did not have breakfast till 9.0 – table d'hôte at 9.0 – so we had the coffee room to ourselves with the exception of "Spats". Started by "Prince of Wales" coach at 9.0 – from Royal Hotel door. Had the three box seats. The driver a splendid old man – driven the Queen for 30 years, & knew them all well. Through a quite pastoral country – Blairgowrie where we waited some time by Anderson's Royal Hotel – I looked round. A very nice girl got up there – was going to Mr. Paterson's of Scott at — Castle on the way. Changed horses twice. Got to Invercauld Hotel at Spital of Glenshee at about 3.0. It got fearfully cold & I was terribly hungry. All had lunch – 20 minutes allowed. On again afterwards – cold increased. We went on mounting & mounting till at the Devil's Elbow we were 2200 ft. above sea level. The horses had quite a scramble to get up. I shivered, although myself quite a bundle of rugs! The country had quite changed, was very wild & rugged, & all heather & juniper bushes. Dull & still colder till at last we got in sight of Braemar & very thankful I was. Coach stopped at Fife Arms, where we had rooms. They were absolutely full – turned some away. "Spats" had to have a drawing room shakedown. Our rooms small – & far apart – about ¼ of a mile! quite a confusion rounds. Had tea about 2.30

Thursday 18th

Had a treat & did not have breakfast till 8.0 - table d'hôte at 9.0 - so we had the coffee room to ourselves with the exception of "Spats". Started by "Prince of Wales" coach at 9.0 - from Royal Hotel door. Had the three box seats. The driver, a splendid old man - driven the Queen for 30 years & knew them all well. Through a quite pastoral country - Blairgowrie, where we waited some time by Anderson's Royal Hotel - & looked round. A very nice girl got up there. Was going to Mr Paterson's of Scith at — Castle on the way. Changed horses twice. Got to Invercauld Hotel at Spital of Glenshee at about 3.0. It got fearfully cold & I was terribly hungry. All had lunch - 20 minutes allowed. On again afterwards - cold increased, we went on mounting & mounting till at the Devil's Elbow we were 2200 ft. above sea level. The horses had quite a scramble to get up. I shivered, although myself quite a bundle of rugs! The country had quite changed, was very wild & rugged, & all heather & juniper bushes. Dull & still colder till at last we got in sight of Braemar & very thankful I was. Coach stopped at Fife Arms, where we had rooms. They were absolutely full - turned some away, "Spats" had to have a drawing room shakedown. Our rooms small & far apart - about 1/4 of a mile! Quite a confusing journey. Had tea about 7.30.

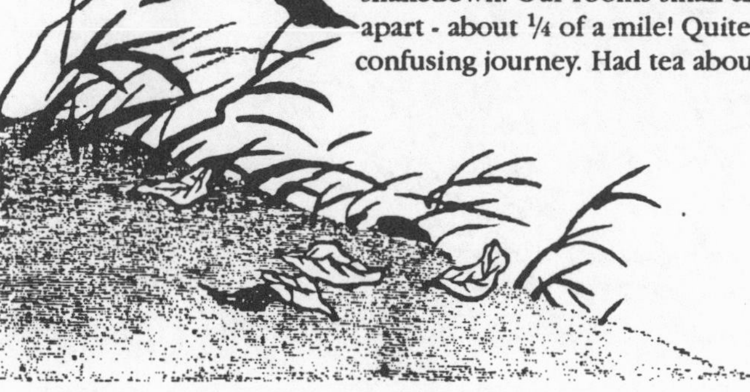

afterwards Papa & I went a little stroll towards Deeside, & met the little "spats". Went also to inspect the "Invercauld" – a very nice hotel. A Scotch piper playing in front & the waiters in kilts. The visitors principally people from London & Kent. Came in & sat in Writing Room & wrote up diary.

Friday. 19th.

Had a very lazy day. Mother not at all well, so she went to the doctor after breakfast, & he ordered her to stay indoors all day. Papa & I had a walk before breakfast by the side of the river. After 9.0. breakfast settled Mother in the drawing room for the day, & I took my painting things, & Papa & I went off a walk & hoping to get a time for painting. We first of all started off little "spats", the poor little man, was tired of the bed on the drawing room floor & went off by the first coach. We walked to the Corromulzie Falls. Two heavy showers came down, so we sat under a tree, & I tried to draw something through the mist, not very successful. Met a lot of nice people at the Falls. Walked home after waiting a little. The road seemed positively endless, but we got to the hotel about 3.0. I sat

Afterwards Papa & I went a little stroll towards Deeside & met the little "Spats". Went also to inspect the "Invercauld" - a very nice hotel. A Scotch piper playing in front & the waiters in kilts. The visitors principally people from London & Kent. Came in & sat in Writing Room & wrote up diary.

Friday 19th

Had a very lazy day. Mother not at all well, so she went to the doctor after breakfast & he ordered her to stay indoors all day. Papa & I had a walk before breakfast by the side of the river. After 9.0 breakfast, settled Mother in the drawing room for the day, & I took my painting things, & Papa & I went off a walk, I hoping to get a time for painting. We first of all started off little "Spats", he poor little man, was tired of the bed on the drawing room floor & went off by the first coach. We walked to the Coromulzie Falls. Two heavy showers came down, so we sat under a tree, & I tried to draw something through the mist, not very successful. Met a lot of nice people at the Falls. Walked home after waiting a little. The road seemed positively endless, but we got to the hotel about 3.0 - I sat

in my room, & had a little refreshment, & then dropped off to sleep till 5.30. Got dressed for dinner, only Papa & myself - Mother did not go, but stayed by herself in the drawing room. After dinner when the Prince had come in Papa & I went another little stroll, & bought some photos. etc. Came in & took chair in drawing room in a circle of dowagers - very nice people. Last night slept my door open to hear the songs from the drawing room & they finished up with God save the Queen. To-night there is a concert here & many people have gone.

Saturday. 20th. - Did not go a walk before breakfast, but packed up instead. Saw the whole of the Prince's party, except himself. Made final preparations & saw final adieus - & then were ready to start at 10.15 by the coach for Ballater. Had splendid seats - at first a great crush, but some people got off at Balmoral & left us the seats to ourselves. A very entertaining man from Chatham got a the box at the Invercauld & subsequently travelled all the way to Aberdeen with us. Had a splendid drive from Braemar to Ballater - 18 miles - past Queen's drive, Balmoral - & Abergeldie &c. Had 1½ hours to wait for our train at Ballater, - so had lunch & got warm. The entertaining man was most amusing & a great acquisition. Took train from Ballater to Aberdeen & only in my room, & had a little refreshment, & then dropped off to sleep till 5.30. Got dressed for dinner, only Papa & myself, Mother did not go, but stayed by herself in the drawing room. After dinner when the Prince had come in Papa & I went another little stroll, & bought some photos etc. Came in & wrote diary in drawing room in a circle of dowagers - very nice people. Last night I left my door open to hear the songs from the drawing room, & they finished up with God Save the Queen. To-night there is a concert here & many people have gone.

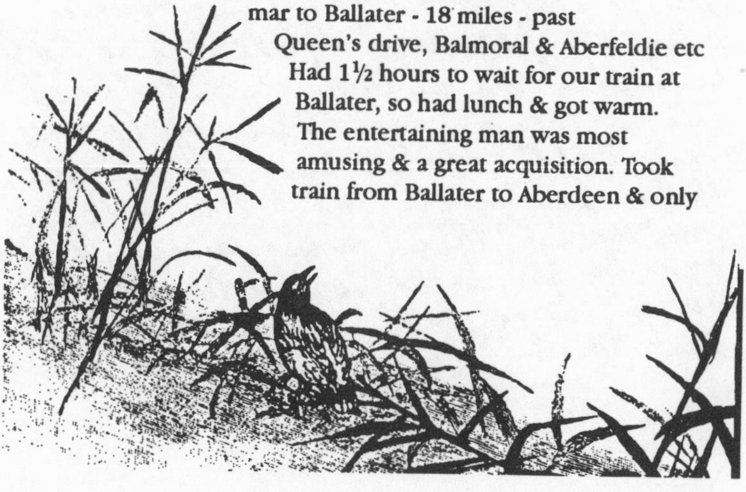

Saturday 20th. Did not go a walk before 9.0. breakfast, but packed up instead. Saw the whole of the Prince's party, except himself. Made final preparations & said final adieus - & then were ready to start at 10.15 by the coach for Ballater. Had splendid seats - at first a great crush, but some people got off at Balmoral & left us the seats to ourselves. A very entertaining man from Chatham got on the box at the Invercauld & subsequently travelled all the way to Aberdeen with us. Had a splendid drive from Braemar to Ballater - 18 miles - past Queen's drive, Balmoral & Aberfeldie etc Had 1½ hours to wait for our train at Ballater, so had lunch & got warm. The entertaining man was most amusing & a great acquisition. Took train from Ballater to Aberdeen & only had about 5 minutes to change train in Perth, as our train was late. Just managed it however, & got into the longest train I ever saw. Hurried the guard on, because of the little time allowed at Perth & eventually had plenty of time there. Changed train again & got into train for Dunkeld with a Warwickshire lady & husband (!?) (mighty hangs a tale!) Awfully hungry & tired. Got to Dunkeld about 8.30. Went straight to Fisher's Royal & had dinner as soon as possible. Then in drawing room, reading & talking till so sleepy, that I had to go to bed. Some awfully nice people staying in the hotel over Sunday.

Sunday 21st:

Up very late, as breakfast not till 9.30! Dawdled rather over it. Afterwards Mother went to the Cathedral. Papa & I set off for a walk. Found our way out 3 miles to the Rumbling Bridge & the Falls of Braan, & found also the proprietor of the same, who unlocked the entrances & let us in. Magnificent falls, only of course very little water in — Sat admiring them for nearly an hour, — Papa smoking, then commenced to retrace our steps. Went round another way, hoping to get to the Hermitage Falls, but found they were private property.

had about 5 minutes to change trains for Perth, as our train was late. Just managed it, however, & got into the longest train I ever saw. Hurried the guard on, because of the little time allowed at Perth & eventually had plenty of time there. Changed trains again & got into train for Dunkeld with a Warwickshire lady & husband (thereby hangs a tale). Awfully hungry & tired. Got to Dunkeld about 8.30 went straight to Fisher's Royal & had dinner as soon as possible. Then in drawing room, reading & talking, till so sleepy that I had to go to bed. Some awfully nice people staying in the hotel over Sunday.

Sunday 21st

Up very late, as breakfast not till 9.30! Dawdled rather over it. Afterwards Mother went to the Cathedral & Papa & I set off for a walk - Found our way out 3 miles to the Rumbling Bridge & the Falls of Bran, & found also the proprietor of the same, who unlocked the entrances & let us in. Magnificent falls, only of course very little water in - sat admiring them for nearly an hour - Papa smoking, then commenced to retrace our steps. Went round another way, hoping to get to the Hermitage falls but found they were private property.

Got rather tired — it was so hot — & kind of dragged home to the hotel. Reposed in jolly arm chair in drawing room & read "World" then had milk & biscuits, & we all three went out, & having found a guide walked round the Dowager Duchess of Athole's grounds. Very extensive & the most lovely trees — so high. The guide was terribly uncommunicative & uplifted, so we did not get much out of him. Just back in time for dinner at 5.0. — Began wrote a letter. Immediately after dinner Papa & I went off to the Presbyterian service at the Cathedral, & found it funny but liked it. Sat in a square pew, with a table in it. & the singing man, sang in the highest pew possible. The sermon or discourse was so long, I was glad when it was over. Walked home. & wrote my diary up in the drawing room. A gay old gentleman came up & talked to us, & also his friend — a "funny man". A long & amusing argument which kept us up till after 11.0 — the latest on record.

Monday. 22nd

Had breakfast with the early coach people — in order to go out & get some photos. Watched the coach start. To our sorrow it commenced to rain, when our turn came to start & as it turned out — our one wet day set in. Started from

Got rather tired - it was so hot & kind of dragged home to the hotel. Reposed in jolly arm chair in drawing room & read "World", then had milk & biscuits, & we all three went out, & having found a guide, walked round the Dowager Duchess of Athole's grounds. Very extensive & the most lovely trees - so high. The guide was terribly uncommunicative & uplifted, so we did not get much out of him. Just back in time for dinner at 5.0. Began to write a letter. Immediately after dinner Papa & I went off to the Presbyterian service at the Cathedral, & found it funny, but liked it. Sat in a square pew, with a table in it, & the singing man, sang in the highest pew possible. The sermon or discourse was so long I was glad when it was over. Walked home, & wrote my diary up in the drawing room. A gay old gentleman came up & talked to us, & also his friend - a "funny man". A long & amusing argument which kept us up till after 11.0 - the latest on record.

Monday 22nd

Had breakfast with the early coach people = in order to go out & get some photos. Watched the coach start. To our sorrow it commenced to rain, when our turn came to start, & as it turned out - our one wet day set in. Started from the hotel at 9.40, & by the 10.0 train for Aberfeldy. Changed at Ballinluig Junction & then at Aberfeldy where we got on to the coach. The funny man & his friend going the same way, travelled with us. A very dismal & wet drive for 5 miles to Kenmore at the head of Loch Tay, where we got the steamer "Lady of the Lake". Everyone's umbrella during the drive ran down everyone else's back & the result was eminently depressing. On the steamer, the most of the scenery of Loch Tay I saw through the saloon windows. Had lunch on board. At Killin the other end of the Lake, got on to the train & at Killin Junction changed into the train for Callender. Reached there about 4.30. Rain has ceased, & on a coach all to ourselves we drove to the Trossachs Hotel, through the Trossachs, & were just in time for table d'hôte at 6.0. During dinner much interested in the N.M.Cs, especially one. Walked in grounds & then spent a busy evening writing & doing album in drawing room.

Tuesday. 23rd.

Ryan Take. A pouring wet morning which almost decided us to stop a'day at the Trossachs – Our coach was the hotel at 9.40, & by the 10.0 train for Aberfeldy. Changed at Ballinluig Junction & then at Aberfeldy, where we got on to the coach. The funny man & his friend going the same way, travelled with us. A very dismal & wet drive for 5 miles to Kenmore at the head of Loch Tay, where we got the steamer "Lady of the Lake". Everyone's umbrella during the drive ran down everyone else's back & the result was eminently depressing. On the steamer, the most of the scenery of Loch Tay, I saw through the saloon windows. Had lunch on board. At Killin the other end of the lake, got on to the train & at Killin Junction changed into the train for Callender. Reached there about 4.50. Rain has ceased, so on a coach all to ourselves we drove to the Trossachs Hotel, through the Trossachs, and were just in time for table d'hôte at 6.0. During dinner much interested in the N.M.Cs, especially one. Walked in grounds & then spent a busy evening writing & doing album in drawing room.

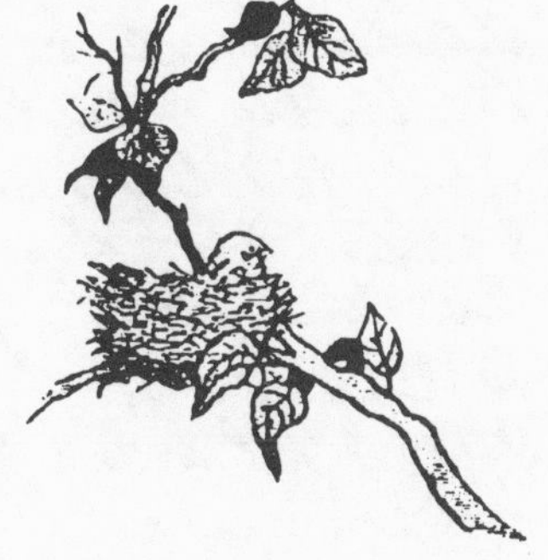

Tuesday 23rd

Again late. A pouring wet morning which almost decided us to stop all day at the Trossachs - our coach was timed to start about 11.0 & almost exactly then, the rain cleared up wonderfully & we had no more all day. Drove from the hotel to the head of Loch Katrine – 1½ miles away & there got on the steamer, & went away down the lake by Ellen's Isle & Silver Strand to Stronachlachen at the other end. Here we got coaches – I managed to have a box seat – & we drove 5 miles to Inversnaid on Loch Lomond. Here we found a confused medley of passengers & luggage, & failing to get milk contented ourselves with milk & a sandwich at the bar. Got on to steamer Prince Consort & went down to the bottom of the lake to Balloch, calling on the way at Tarbet & two other places. Here the train stood waiting on the pier, so we took places & went through to Glasgow, calling however at most places en route – At Glasgow we changed for Edinburgh & got there a little after 6.0 – after a quick run. Travelled with 3 nice women from Chicago who knew W.S.K. very well – & many other mutual friends we discovered. 4 wheeler from station to Balmoral Hotel. Found letters from both timed to start about 11.0 & almost exactly then, the rain cleared up wonderfully & we had no more all day. Drove from the hotel to the head of Loch Katrine - 1½ miles away & there got on the steamer, & went away down the lake by Ellen's Isle & Silver Strand to Stronachlachar at the other end. Here we got coaches - I managed to have a box seat - & we drove 5 miles to Inversnaid on Loch Lomond. Here we found a confused medley of passengers & luggage, & failing to get milk contented ourselves with milk & sandwich at the bar. Got on to steamer Prince Consort & went down to the bottom of the lake to Balloch, calling on the way at Tarbet & two other places. Here the train stood waiting on the pier. So we took places & went through to Glasgow, calling however at most places en route - At Glasgow we changed for Edinburgh & got there a little after 6.0 - after a quick run. Travelled with 3 nice women from Chicago who knew Mr K. very well - & many other mutual friends, we discovered. 4 wheeler from station to Balmoral Hotel. Found letters from both

boys waiting me. Dressed & waited for 8.0. table d'hôte. Afterwards, Mother & father a walk in Princes St. by gaslight – I in drawing room to write. Heat here so great, & different to the cold at Balmoral & the Highlands.

Wednesday 24th –

There is an end to all things, but an abrupt ending to say the least unpleasant. While dressing 2 telegrams came, to say fire at the Mill. Of course, not knowing the extent, we were in a terrible state of consternation. Got telegrams at 9.0 – were in the flying Scotchman by 10.0, had our breakfasts & packed &c in meantime. I had quite a big lump in my throat, it was so sad to leave Edinburgh looking so lovely. Had intended to get photos, tartans, & many things! Had carriage to ourselves nearly all the way. Lunched at Preston. At Crewe got paper with account of fire, which plunged us all again into gloom. Saw wreck from train. Got to New Street about 6.45. Straight home. Had tea. Then Papa rushed off at once to inspect the remains. I sadly & slowly unpacked my much squashed luggage –

boys waiting me. Dressed & waited for 8.0. table d'hôte. Afterwards, mother & father a walk in Princes St. by gaslight - I in drawing room to write. Heat here so great & different to the cold at Braemar & the Highlands.

Wednesday 24th

There is an end to all things, but an abrupt ending is to say the least unpleasant. While dressing 2 telegrams came, to say Fire at the Mill. Of course, not knowing the extent, we were in a terrible state of consternation. Got telegrams at 9.0 - were in the flying Scotchman by 10.0, had our breakfasts & packed etc. in meantime. I had quite a big lump in my throat, it was so sad to leave Edinburgh looking so lovely. Had intended to get photos, tartans, & many things! Had carriage to ourselves nearly all the way. Lunched at Preston. At Crewe got paper with account of fire - which plunged us all again into gloom. Saw wreck from train. Got to New Street about 6.45. Straight home & had tea. Then Papa rushed off at once to inspect the remains - & I sadly & slowly unpacked my much squashed luggage -

The old young men.
DRIVER.

Through the saloon window.
Den at the wheel.
The young man on the cabin stairs.
Fancy portrait.
Old milkseller at Fort Augustus

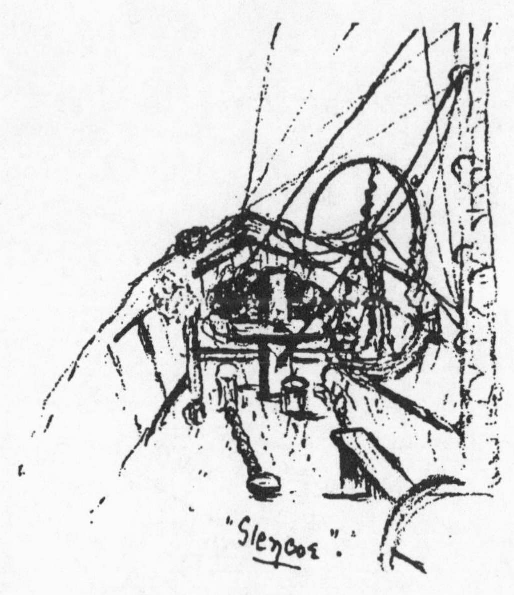
"Glencoe".

All that was seen of the ladys maid
Charming old lady in a windy corner.
Captain?

R.F.
Back
Awe

No. of Message..............................

POST OFFICE TELEGRAPHS.

HARRISON & SONS, LONDON.

If the accuracy of an Inland Telegram be doubted, the telegram will be repeated on payment of half the amount originally paid for its transmission, any fraction of 1d. less than ½d. being reckoned as ½d.; and if it be found that there was any inaccuracy, the amount paid for repetition will be refunded. Special conditions are applicable to the repetition of Foreign Telegrams.

N.B.—This Form must accompany any inquiry made respecting this Telegram.

Dated Stamp of Delivering Office. GLASGOW AU

Charges to pay £............s..........d.

Handed in at the Birmingham Office at [illegible] M. Received here at [illegible] M.

TO [illegible] of Birmingham Central Hotel [illegible]

Welcome to [illegible] [illegible] [illegible] Comfortable

The twelve-word, sixpenny telegram from Marie's brothers

SERIOUS FIRE AT A BIRMINGHAM FLOUR MILL.

About one o'clock this morning a fire broke out at the extensive flour mills belonging to Messrs. Watson, Todd, and Watson, situate in St. Vincent Street, Ladywood. For some time past the mills have been at work night and day, and at the hour named Caleb Plater, the man in charge of the wheat cleaning department, observed smoke issuing from one of the rooms under his control. The premises are of considerable size, being the largest in the district, and the machinery is of the latest and most improved kind. The building, which is the shape of the letter L, was erected some eighteen years ago, and ten years since a wing was added, and this was used for the cleaning of the wheat, the machinery being of a special character. The premises are six storeys high, and are bounded on one side by St. Vincent Street, and others by the canal and railway. The wing where the fire broke out is situated near the latter. It is customary each day to remove the dust from the cleaning rooms, and this was done yesterday. Three rooms are devoted to the cleaning machinery, while in the rooms above are stored the wheat about to be operated on. The main granary is situated in that portion of the factory immediately abutting on the wing, and communicating with it by several doors, the latter being of iron. Plater, it appears, had left the machinery for a few moments while he went into the upper storeys, and then everything appeared perfectly safe. When he returned, however, the cleaning-rooms were filled with dense smoke. He raised an alarm, and steps were at once taken to acquaint the fire-brigade authorities. The whole brigade, under Captain Tozer, were speedily on the spot with the steamer, manual engine, and other appliances, and about the same time, or a little before, the fire-escape from the Ladywood Police Station was brought on the scene. Jets were at once attached to the mains, and steps taken to bring the steamer into operation. The water for the latter was obtained from the canal, and some unavoidable delay occurred before the steamer could be got to work, owing to a way having to be cut through the barrier (consisting of old railway sleepers) separating the canal from the firm's premises to allow the steamer to be placed on the canal bank. Up to this time very little flame was to be seen, and to the spectators who had assembled it seemed as though the fire had been practically extinguished. Unfortunately, however, this was not the case. Dense smoke began to issue from the numerous windows of the cleaning rooms, and occasionally there were flashes of flame. In a short time it became evident that the three lower storeys were alight, and strenuous efforts were made by the brigade to stay the further progress of the fire, but this was a work of considerable difficulty, owing to the depth of the rooms, which are some sixteen yards wide, and, perhaps, twenty yards or so deep. The pressure of the water both from the mains and from the steamer was everything that could be wished for, but it soon became clear that the fire had got too firm a hold to be readily extinguished, and flames were observed in the storey immediately over those in which the cleaning machinery was in. Masses of flame came bursting through the numerous windows, and a few seconds later extended to the two storeys above, the entire wing being then one mass of fire, the flames darting high in the heavens, accompanied by large clouds of sparks, resembling an immense pyrotechnic display. Speedily the roof fell in, and was followed by the floors. It was wonderful how long the latter held together, and it was at first believed that they were of concrete, but enquiry led to the discovery that they were of elm. Just before the roof collapsed the escape from the Council House was brought to the mill, it having been sent for by Superintendent Tozer, the one from the Ladywood Police Station being too small to be of much use. The Council House escape is of great height, and when reared against the burning mill it was found to reach some distance above the roof. Up the escape firemen mounted, and from that lofty position poured a steady stream of water on the flames. At the same time a couple of hose pipes were attached to one nozzle, and the stream of water thus delivered on the burning building rivalled in force the one from the steamer. So great, indeed, was the force of this concentrated stream that the nozzle was rested on an iron stand, and held by two firemen. During the progress of the fire the Aston brigade arrived on the scene, and rendered valuable assistance, as did also Mitchell's brigade at a later period. At the time of going to press the fire was still burning; but the volume of water which was being poured on it by the three brigades was such as to justify the belief that it would in course of an hour or so be put out, and that the main portion of the building would be saved. During the time the cleaning department was burning furiously, the rest of the mill was kept at work, and not until the arrival of one of the partners were operations suspended, and the boiler fires drawn. As to the cause of the fire nothing is at present known; but it was suggested by several workmen that it was due to the over-heating of some of the bearings. It is understood that the loss is covered by insurance. A large force of police was present at the fire, but there was little for them to do, the crowd which had assembled being perfectly orderly and good tempered.

Contemporary report, found in the diary, of the fire at Watson, Todd & Watson, Marie's father's flour mill

V

A COMMENTARY ON MARIE'S DIARY

V

A COMMENTARY ON MARIE'S DIARY

(1) *West Ham House and Cambridge*

The aim of this holiday was to proceed to West Ham House, stay overnight there with the Buck family, and join with Mrs Buck and one of her daughters on a trip to Cambridge, where one of her sons was an undergraduate. The Buck household consisted of Irish-born William Richard, secretary of the Shipwrecked Mariners' Society, 49, his 43-year-old wife, Alice Emmeline, a Londoner, their six boys aged 6 to 23 and four girls aged 12 to 21, a nursemaid, a housemaid and a cook. The daughter joining the Cambridge trip was Edith Beatrice, two months younger than Marie. She, however, preferred the name Mabel to either of the two names she had been given, so she is called Mabel throughout the diary and her autograph appears there as Mabel Buck. She and Marie had both lived at Myra Lodge as boarders with Miss Buss (to whose dance they were all now going at her invitation after they reached Cambridge); and Annie Maude Howard, eight months younger than Marie, daughter of George Howard (a manufacturer living at Oakwood, Cricklewood) who had been a *day* pupil at the North London Collegiate, joined the Cambridge-bound group at Liverpool Street Station.

Of the other members of the Buck family, Percy Carter, with whom she went to 'an amusing concert', and whose organ playing she described as 'splendid' on a later occasion, afterwards had a highly successful musical career. Most of the boys went to Merchant Taylors, referred to in the diary by the letters 'MT'. Though the name West Ham House might suggest the dwelling of a well-to-do manufacturer or professional man, its situation in West Ham Lane, number 58, next door to the 'British Lion' public house, probably reflects the constraints imposed by the small salary paid to officials of voluntary organisations. It is to Marie's credit that no hint of any adverse comparison of West

Ham Lane with Calthorpe Road is given in her diary.

On their arrival at Cambridge they were met by Willie, 23-year-old William Armstrong Buck, of Peterhouse. Lunch was in Trinidad-born Harry Stanley Branscombe's rooms in St John's. He was the same age as Willie, and both of them became clergymen. The event of the day was, however, the dance in the evening organised by 60-year-old Miss Buss. 'During her nephews' college careers she several times took a house at Cambridge, always arranging something in which her girl-undergraduates could join.' At the dance given the previous year jointly by Miss Buss and Mrs Mathieson the latter tells us,

> I think we had about twenty from Girton, and the same number from Newnham, and Miss Hughes brought about twelve from the Training College. Miss Buss and I each took down a party, and there were plenty of men from the various colleges.

On the 1887 occasion Marie's partners included James Francis, Mrs Mathieson's son; Reginald James Fletcher of Peterhouse, whose brother Bertram's violin playing Marie listened to later (he went on to become violin master at Rugby and Uppingham); William Elliott Drake, Clare (who afterwards practised as a doctor and later went to Australia); and James Elliott Mallinson, Sidney, who became a solicitor.

The following day they also saw something of John Carpenter Turner (Cavendish House), who went down, Marie tells us, on June 16th. Like many of the other students she encountered on her Cambridge visits, he was destined for the Church. So was Arthur Clement Buss, Pembroke, the younger brother of Francis Fleetwood Buss, also Pembroke; they were the sons of Septimus Buss, Vicar of Shoreditch, and therefore nephews of Miss Buss. To round off the day, the strains of 'The Place where the Old Horse Died' came through the window of Marie's room. This hunting song, published in 1882, the first line being 'In the Hollow, by the Pollard', no doubt owed part of its Cambridge popularity to having a chorus *ad lib.* (giving ample scope for mock exaggerated grief).

Sunday's events included a visit to Girton, where she was shown round by a resident science lecturer, Maria Mabel Anelay, who had herself been a student there eight years earlier. Marion Bessie Mathieson, (a day pupil at the North London Collegiate), whose room was so much admired, was almost exactly the same age as Marie. She was the daughter of Frederic Coxhead Mathieson (a Hampstead publisher) and the Mrs Mathieson on whom Marie called on May 12th during one of her London visits, and was the sister of James Francis, one of Marie's partners at Miss Buss's Cambridge dance. Marion married Sydney Wales, a

London solicitor, ten years later, and became active in social work and education in the Hampstead area. In the ten years from 1877 to 1886, the North London Collegiate School had contributed 15 out of a total Girton intake of 199, so roughly seven and a half per cent of all the girls who became students at Girton in that decade had been pupils of Miss Buss.

HONOUR TO AGNATA FRANCES RAMSAY!
CAMBRIDGE, JUNE 1887
Drawn by George du Maurier

Cartoon from Punch, *June 1887*

It was at the time of Marie's *next* visit to Cambridge, however, that the success of one Girton girl became the subject of a Punch cartoon and so aroused national interest. Agnata Frances Ramsay was the only candidate in the whole University to achieve a first class in the Classical

Tripos. Her sex would in fact have precluded her from wearing the gown in which she is shown being ushered by Mr Punch into a 'Ladies Only' first-class carriage, but such a detail did not detract from the excitement of the occasion.

(2) *Cambridge, Second Edition*

One of the few people whom she had not encountered on her previous visit who can be positively identified is John Lionel Shirley Dampier Bennett, Emmanuel. As he had been at MT, and was the son of the Vicar of St Paul's, South Hampstead, Marie may well have met him earlier, in her schooldays. There were two Hancocks (Herbert, St John's, and Leonard Rhys, Peterhouse), either of whom could have been the one she saw on both her Cambridge visits, and both of them became clergymen. On Friday 17th June, Hancock and someone whose name seems to have five letters beginning with 'S' (could it be Shilt?) joined the breakfast Marie had with Arthur Buss; but though he is mentioned several times, it does not seem possible to make a positive identification. Barley was probably Charles Vere Barley, St Catherine's; and Roper may have been Henry Roper, Christ's.

(3) *London*

The London holiday started at West Ham House on Tuesday 10th May, Marie, Mabel and Mrs Buck having returned from the first Cambridge trip on the Monday evening. On Tuesday afternoon there was boating on the lake in Wanstead Park, travelling there by omnibus and back again by tram (also horse-drawn, of course). Then on the afternoon of Wednesday 11th May, Marie set forth on what was always a rather awkward journey to Myra Lodge. It may seem a little odd that soon after her arrival there Marie, who was on holiday, should have gone with Maude Howard and some of the girls to the dinner and after-dinner speeches of the Governesses' Benevolent Institution, which might sound neither an entertaining nor even a particularly educational event. There were, however, rather special reasons for going. For when, back in 1848, the GBI had been given a Royal Charter enabling it to found Queen's College, Miss Buss, who was at that time teaching during the day, was then able to attend evening classes at this new college. So that, in addition to seeking to improve the *conditions* of governesses in every way, the GBI aimed to encourage women generally, particularly those who undertook such work, to improve their educational qualifications. And the NLCS girls will undoubtedly have heard from Miss Buss on many occasions how important a role the GBI had played, and was still playing, in the campaign to improve the education and working conditions of middle-class women.

The impression conveyed by Marie's references to Miss Buss in the 1887 Diary is very much like the description Sara Burstall gives of her in the same year. She was

> sixty in age, but in appearance and in bodily strength much what women of eighty are now [1938], but she went on with her work and her outside interests as buoyantly and resolutely as ever.

In fact, unlike many of her pioneer women contemporaries, who lived to unusually advanced ages, Frances Mary Buss, literally worn out by the exertions of her working life, only lived some seven years after Queen Victoria's Jubilee, dying at merely 67 in December 1894.

Marie Todd, Maude and Miss Fawcett went on May 13th to 'German Reed's and saw the Naturalist . . .' This may need some elucidation. Thomas German Reed, musician and entertainer, had the lease of St George's Hall, and with his wife Priscilla Horton, their son Alfred, Corney Grain and others, was highly successful for many years in putting on a wide range of operettas.

Going with Maude Howard to her Oaklands, Cricklewood home on Saturday 14th May, Marie was able to get to know Maude's brother Walter (whom she only previously knew by sight), late in the evening, and sat all the following afternoon on the verandah talking to him. Walter Howard was the same age, and later made a name for himself as actor, manager, and dramatist; he died in his mid-fifties. Mr and Mrs Frankau, who came to tea at the Howards on that Sunday, were most probably Arthur Frankau, cigar merchant, and Julia Davies, whom he had married four years before. She was only two years older than Marie, but was already becoming quite well known in London literary circles (under the name Frank Danby), both as a journalist and as a novelist. And after they left, Marie started to read *Zoraster, Thus Spake Nietzsche*, presumably found among Mr Howard's books (she finished it the following day); and, perhaps surprisingly for a girl of her age, found it 'splendid'. She might well be surprised and pleased to know that his teachings, of so many centuries before she read about them, were going still, a century later, to form the *raison d'être* for small but dedicated groups of followers in many countries, including Britain.

On at least two occasions during the Myra section of her London holiday, Marie showed remarkable helpfulness to friends in trouble. Thus on Monday 16th May a letter reached her from Willie Buck asking her if she could fetch some things for him, so she abandoned any other plans she might have had and journeyed to West Ham to deal with the matter, returning to Myra late in the evening. And on the following day, when Miss Buss developed a bad cold making it difficult for her to cope with her Tuesday afternoon 'At Home', Marie very decently resisted any temptation to go out and enjoy herself and stayed at Myra instead to help until the last caller had gone. No wonder that when in the evening she and Miss Fawcett were returning from the 'Lady Clancarty' performance, she dozed in a shaky omnibus; she might have slept more soundly had pneumatic tyres been invented then.

Marie stayed in yet another part of London when she went to visit her school friend Susie Bray and her family. Edward Bray, Susie's father, was incumbent of St Saviour's, Poplar, when he applied for his daughter's admission to the NLCS. He had now moved a few miles westwards, so Marie's visit to them starting on Monday 23rd May, obviously a most enjoyable one, was to the Rectory, Shadwell. Susie was only some seven months younger than Marie. She both played the violin and sang. The account of her performance at an Old Pupils' Meeting a year later speaks of 'Miss Susie Bray's appropriate song, "Fiddle and I"'; on the same occasion she also sang 'The Old and the Young Marie'. Although Marie Todd's own wedding did not take place until she was over 27 years old, at the marriages of two of her school friends—Susie Bray's to George Sargent and Mary Mathieson's to Sydney Wales—the brides were in their thirties.

In addition to seeing a good deal of Miss Buss, Miss Caroline Fawcett and Miss Sarah Ann Paul on her London holiday, Marie also called on a number of others who had taught her or whom she knew from her Myra days. The Miss Ridley she visited on Friday 20th May was probably Jane Taylor Ridley who acted as honorary secretary of the Cambridge Local Examinations held at Sandall Road, where the candidates came exclusively from Miss Buss's schools. Jeannie, as she was known, was the younger sister of Miss Annie Eleanor Ridley who had been a Governor of the NLCS from the beginning and who afterwards wrote the 1895 biography of Frances Mary Buss. Two days before calling on Miss Ridley, Marie had visited Miss Henrietta C. Brooks. And that same evening she tells us that 'Nellie and I had drawing room alone'—Nellie was Miss E.M. Childs, whom one former pupil described as being 'always a pleasure to listen to'.

But this does not exhaust the number of teachers she must have seen on this holiday visit, for quite a number whom she does not mention in the diary nevertheless provided her with autographs. These included the Rev. Edward L. Cutts (who used to give the Wednesday Bible Address), Miss Eleanor Begbie (Superintendent), Miss Mary Tiffin (solo singing), and Miss Jane Marchant—perhaps she met some of them again at the Old Pupils' Meeting she reports going to on Wednesday 25th May.

(4) *Comberford (a hamlet on the river Tame)*

The distinguishing feature of this holiday was that she went to stay with relatives, and that they and their friends were nearly all farmers. Henry Lowe, her uncle, had married Marie's father's sister, Anne. He himself, a farmer with large water mills at Comberford, had died a year ago, and as the second day of Marie's visit was the anniversary of his death, she and her Auntie Anne drove to the four-acre cemetery on the Wigginton Road, opened eleven years before. They then went on to Windmill Farm where Tom Lowe, his wife Emily, and his daughter Florrie lived. At Elford, on the following day, the wife of William Cripwell, another farmer, was called on. And Charles Coxon and his wife, to whom they then drove on, were also farmers in Elford. Yet another farming family, that of Thomas Cheatle of Mountside House, Dosthill, was visited for tea next day; and Lizzie and Charlie, who came over for supper, were farmers as well; they were the Lowes from Whateley Hall. Among the people she met, only the wealthy William Barmingham, George Shaw, the Clarsons and Mrs Frances Parson, all from Tamworth and district, seem not to have been currently engaged in that activity.

(5) *Langley Priory, Leicestershire*

This was essentially a 'stately homes' holiday, far removed from anything even the urban wealth of Edgbaston could offer. From the moment of alighting from the train at Tonge station (one and a half miles from the Priory), on the branch line between Derby and Ashby-de-la-Zouch, she moved into a different world. It was still a different world even for the family *living* at Langley Priory, for Charles Shakespear, the head of the household, had been born Charles Bowles, but by the 1858 Will of his maternal uncle, John Shakespear, had assumed the name of Shakespear and acquired Langley, which at 48 was quite a move up in the world for him; he had previously earned a very modest living as Professor of Hindustani in the East India Company's College at Addiscombe, Croydon.

The Priory, founded about 1100 for Benedictine nuns, had some time after its dissolution in 1535 been replaced by a mansion built on the site, with 'a fine sheet of water in front, and surrounded by undulating woodland scenery', the acreage being variously given as 564 or 1,716. Charles Shakespear, now 76, and his 55-year-old wife Elizabeth had, since moving into Langley Priory, had five daughters and two sons; but John, who would have been 18, had died the year before Marie's visit, so that the heir was now 17-year-old Charles Bowles Shakespear. So if Marie's remark 'all at home to meet me' is to be taken literally, this would mean the parents, the heir, and five girls ranging in age from 20 to 26. Gertie, the same age as Marie, was often her companion on walks, but she also saw quite a lot of Ina (probably 20-year-old Selina) and 25-year-old Connie, while 23-year-old Emily Tuck took pride of place on Marie's page devoted to Shakespear autographs.

At Diseworth, the Vicar was the Rev. Arthur Walker, and 'the one shop' was kept by James Roper. William Dashwood Fane of Melbourne Hall (where they went to a tennis party) also owned Fulbeck Hall in Lincolnshire, and was a 71-year-old barrister. The Melbourne Hall gardens

> are in the Dutch style introduced by William III and consist of groves intersecting each other, ornamented with statues and fountains; in one part the yew trees form an alley 80 yards in length from which the light is almost excluded [the tunnel Marie talks of]; the banks of the Great Pool, a lake of about 20 acres in extent, are beautifully wooded and overlooked by terraces which command extensive views of the neighbourhood.

The Briggs, with whom they had a picnic the next day, lived at Bleak House, Kings Newton.

(6) *Scotland*

Marie's holiday with her parents in Scotland differs in one important respect from all her other excursions in 1887. For as they stayed in hotels and not with friends or relatives, it is not necessary to give background information about the hosts, nor about those she encountered when visiting them. And although it is true that she and her parents were joined at various points on the route by friends who were also on holiday, too little information is given about these particular people to make identification possible. So for this section of the diary, unlike the other ones, *no* supplementary background material is being provided; but as Marie herself supplies details about all the places they visited in Scotland, what she has written about this particular holiday can be understood and enjoyed without commentary of any kind.

(7) *Puzzles*

Two factors—Marie's handwriting, and the diary having been written for herself alone—inevitably lead to a certain number of difficulties. Among names of people, there is the case, already noted, of the Cambridge student whose name has five letters apparently beginning with 'S'. Then there is the coded adjective 'N.M.C.', descriptive of some of the young men (and one clergyman) she saw on her holiday in Scotland. This is probably 'Not Much Cop' despite, or perhaps because of, Miss Buss's strong disapproval of the use of slang; though it might have been 'Catch', not 'Cop'. On her second Cambridge visit on June 15th she mysteriously 'Stole p. and had bit'; while on that same day and at the Peterhouse Ball the previous night, something that might be 'Kittens' is mentioned. After shopping at Whiteleys in London on May 21st she dragged something beginning with 'c', which could have been 'cauldron', home in the rain. And a few days later when returning from an Old Pupils' Meeting on May 25th, 'Walked home with Miss Buss. She came in, while Miss F. . .' Could Miss Fawcett have been making silent but good-humoured fun of Miss Buss's stately entry? And then, on her holiday in Scotland, the last sentence of her account of Wednesday 10th August records 'Met M^{r} and Mrs Pierson - 2 Demuths'.

Baby doll, from Sylvia's Home Journal, *May 1883*

A rather different kind of puzzle arises from her use of the term 'work' on her holidays. Thus at West Ham House on May 11th, 'did work', while at Myra Lodge on May 18th we have 'letters and work'. The other references, at Langley Priory, suggest an answer. On August 2nd 'worked and dressed dolls in schoolroom' and two days later, 'having previously dressed each our doll'. Something else that is a little difficult to explain is that when she tells us, at Cambridge on June 16th, that she 'bought flowers', the words are underlined and following by an exclamation mark. Why was this so unusual? Was it because other people always bought them for her, or were there so many in the Calthorpe Road garden that buying them was usually unnecessary? One other matter mentioned several times in the diary is also difficult to explain—when her friends played tennis, she herself never took part. On Monday 1st August, for instance, 'After dinner had a tennis party at Langley Priory. I of course looked on.' Was she such a bad tennis player that her participation was likely to spoil the game for the others? In that case her insistence on always merely being a spectator is very much to her credit.

VI

AFTER 1887

VI

AFTER 1887

(1) *Life as Mrs Conway Lowe*

So on August 2nd 1893, during a heat wave that cost the life of at least one person locally, Marie Todd married Conway Lowe at St George's Church, Edgbaston, where her father had been prominent as a churchwarden for many years, and where all his children had been baptised. The wedding had been brought forward so that her mother, whose health was failing fast (she died five days afterwards) could be with them. In Marie's account of her holiday in Scotland with her parents six years earlier, there had been frequent mention of her mother not being well enough to participate to the full.

Conway Lowe had been brought up in 'Southfield', 6 Norfolk Road, Edgbaston, a large and impressive house with no less than eight acres of 'ornamental grounds and park-like pasture land' (to quote the description in the advertisement for its subsequent auction on June 9th 1899). His father, Henry Lowe, twenty-four years older than Marie's father, had had seven children (three boys and four girls) in comparison with Marie and her three brothers. Conway himself was the middle boy, and also the middle sibling of his brothers and sisters taken together. He was six years older than Marie, and all his brothers and sisters except one were also older than she was. The two families, the Todds and the Lowes, at 56 Calthorpe Road and 6 Norfolk Road, lived fairly near each other (about a mile and a half apart) in Edgbaston. Henry Lowe, Conway's father, was partner in an old-established and prosperous firm manufacturing saddlers' ironmongery (the range of their products can be seen from the reproduction of their 1880s advertisement). As yet no one could foresee the catastrophic effect that the coming of the internal combustion engine was going to have on the fortunes of a firm such as Lowe, Sleigh, Bevan & Co.

To begin with, Marie and Conway lived at 233 Hagley Road, but about seven years later they moved to 75 Westfield Road, and from there after a similar period they established themselves in 'Eversley', 22 Somerset Road, which was to be their home for thirty-four years or so. This house was only about a mile and a half from 56 Calthorpe Road where Marie had been brought up, and the same distance from 6 Norfolk Road where Conway had lived as a boy. Before this last move, their four children had been born—at 233 Hagley Road, Richard Conway in 1894, Honor Mary in 1897; at 75 Westfield Road, Joyce Burman in 1902 and Henry Conway in 1906. Their association with St George's Church, Edgbaston, continued; Conway became a churchwarden, and all their children were baptised there.

A contemporary photograph of St George's Church, Edgbaston, where Marie's wedding, and the baptism of her four children, took place

'Eversley', the house in Somerset Road which was their home for such a long time, was a very large and impressive one. Not only did it provide space for both a night and a day nursery, and for a domestic staff of five or six, but it also had a lodge accommodating the chauffeur and his wife (Mr and Mrs Johnson stayed on there after Marie and Conway sought refuge in Ham Court in the early part of the Second World War). Each day began with a traditional assembly of family on one side of the table and servants on the other, with Conway leading the prayers and reading a passage from the Bible.

The 1914–18 War brought tragedy to this, as to so many other families. Richard Conway, their eldest son, a Winchester Scholar, a Scholar at Oxford and destined for the Church, joined the Warwickshire Regiment and came back wounded. In January 1916 at an investiture at Bucking-ham Palace, Lieutenant Richard Conway Lowe, 6ft 7in tall, received his Military Cross; and on his return to France later that year, was killed in action on the Somme. The family was naturally devastated.

ESTABLISHED 1747.

LOWE, SLEIGH, BEVAN & CO.,

MANUFACTURERS OF

Coach and Saddlers' Ironmongery.

Carriage and Railway Lamps, Carriage and Harness Mountings, Axletrees, Springs, Beading, and Coach Ironwork, Brass Founders, Bridle Cutters, Saddle Tree, Saddle and Harness Makers, Shippers. Export Merchants, and Railway Contractors.

Inventors and Sole Makers of the Ladies' Patent Carriage Ladderette for Stanhope and Mail Phaetons.

DESIGNERS & SOLE MAKERS of the Registered "Saturn" and "Horse-Shoe" LAMPS.

MANUFACTURERS OF

The "Special" and every other description of Under-Front Carriages.

CLARENCE WORKS,

Offices, Show Room & Warehouse, 69 to 76, CHARLOTTE ST.: Works, 17 & 18 MOTT ST.,

BIRMINGHAM, ENGLAND.

Advertisement in the 1880s of the firm with which Conway Lowe and his father were associated

But Marie, now in her fifties, worked tirelessly in organising women volunteers in Edgbaston for the provision of a laundry service for the Birmingham hospitals desperately trying to cope with the needs of wounded soldiers. In December 1917, when the V.A.D. laundry had completed three years of work, about four thousand articles a week were passing through the hands of its seventy voluntary workers and eight paid laundresses. And, on the fund-raising side of all this, among many successful ventures was a performance on two December evenings, at 'Eversley', of 'The Scarlet Pimpernel', with Marie and her two daughters as major participants.

Conway never really recovered from the loss of his elder son. And when on top of this the family firm, to which he had devoted so much of his life since the 1880s, tried in the 1920s to move over to manufacturing motor car fittings, instead of coach and saddlers' ironmongery, he found himself at odds with his partners on how to adapt, and was bought out. These two blows left Conway a broken man, and Marie had to become the decision maker and mainstay of the family.

(2) *Marie's brothers, nephews and nieces*

It was unusual among Edgbaston fathers to send a *daughter* away to school as a boarder, as Marie's father did. With boys it was different, though the choice of boarding school for Norman and Howard—Trinity College, Glenalmond, Scotland—was a little unexpected. Howard, a stockbroker, remained a bachelor, stayed on at 34 Calthorpe Road after the death of his father in December 1906, and after leaving there in 1939 spent his retirement in Adelaide Cottage, West Malvern. Norman Hill married in 1912, but as as a result of an accident to his wife, they could have no children. In the 1930s he acquired Putley Court, a handsome mansion five miles west of Ledbury in Herefordshire, built in 1712. After the death of his wife in 1939, and in order to keep Putley Court in the Todd family, he decided that on his own death it should be offered first to his brother Howard, then to Richard Stuart and finally to his sister Marie, subject to the provision in each case that the brother or sister concerned should occupy Putley Court as his or her principal place of residence. By the time he himself died in 1949, however, Marie was no longer alive; and as neither Howard nor Richard Stuart apparently availed themselves of the offer, Putley Court was sold and the proceeds divided amongst Norman Hill's nephews and nieces.

It was only through her brother Richard Stuart Todd's marriage to Lilian Mabel Livesey in 1899 that two Todd nephews (Alan Livesey Stuart and Oliver Stuart) and a Todd niece (Lilian Mary Stuart) arrived on the scene for Marie and her other two brothers. Richard Stuart, educated at King Edward's School, Birmingham, was for a time a member of Birmingham City Council. He then lived for some twenty years at Clent Grove, and was High Sheriff of Worcestershire. In the mid-1930s he moved to Woodstock House, Oxfordshire (which, in the language of *Landed Gentry*, was then his 'seat', his 'residence' being Eastcliffe, Budleigh Salterton, Devon).

To round off the story of Marie Todd's nephews and niece, Alan Livesey Stuart, educated at Wellington and Oxford, became a barrister and was an MP for four years in the 1930s (he lost his seat at the 1935 election by only sixteen votes); he took a very active part in the affairs of Worcestershire and lived in the 1970s at Clent House Lodge, near what had been his father's mansion, Clent Grove. By his first wife he had a son Arthur George Stuart Todd, married with children and now in

Australia. Richard Stuart Todd's *second* son Oliver, Squadron-Leader in the RAF, married and had a son Alexander Stuart and four daughters. His wife, Dorothea Janet, remarried and became Mrs Eyre. Finally, Lilian Mary, Richard Stuart Todd's daughter, married Robert William Little, went to Burma and returned to live in Somerset; they had no children.

The situation on Conway's side of the family was very different, as all four of his sisters and both his brothers married and had children. Florence Victoria (the youngest, who was two years younger than Marie) became Mrs Bayfield; Edith Maria, Mrs Jobson; Mary Elizabeth, Mrs Williams; and Eleanor Gertrude, Mrs Panton. In this last case, two of her three sons (whose mother was, of course, a Lowe) also married Lowes with whom we are concerned. Thus Henry Forbes Panton married Marie and Conway's daughter Honor Mary Lowe; while Ian Forbes Panton married Doris Mary Lowe, one of the three daughters of Conway's younger brother, Arthur Labron Lowe; she had previously been married to Captain Philip Dennis Bennett and had a son Dennis Labron and a daughter Phillipa Mary. Conway's *older* brother, Henry Burman Lowe, had two sons, one of whom became Medical Officer of Health for Wiltshire. Conway's *younger* brother, Arthur Labron Lowe, had a very distinguished law career both nationally and in Birmingham. He lived both at 52 Westfield Road and at Monkspath Hall, Shirley.

The explanation of the second of Arthur Labron Lowe's two homes is that a relative, Sarah Jane Farr (née Lowe) had in 1899 left him Monkspath Hall, Shirley, Warwickshire, erected in the early part of the eighteenth century on the site of a mediaeval building. Arthur Labron was living there at the time of his death in 1928. As he was most anxious to keep up the Lowe family connection with the Monkspath Hall estate, and as he himself had three daughters but no son, he directed that on his death it should be offered to his brother Conway (or, if he was no longer living, to Conway's son); and, as an inducement, this was to be at a price twenty-five per cent less than its market valuation. In the event, however, one of his daughters, Marjorie Kathleen, who had married a London solicitor Howard Seys-Phillips, acquired the property. The family connection Arthur Labron Lowe had hoped to maintain was finally broken when in 1975 this Grade 2 listed building passed into the hands of the local authority. In the 1980s a contractor demolishing a barn in the area demolished Monkspath Hall as well but, after a protracted legal battle, had to have it rebuilt, using the original bricks.

(3) *Marie's children and their families*

The oldest of Marie and Conway's three surviving children, Honor Mary, married Henry Forbes Panton, a cousin, one of the three sons of her father's sister, Eleanor Gertrude Panton (née Lowe). Like two of Marie's brothers, he had been to school at Trinity College, Glenalmond. After graduating in Medicine at Edinburgh University in 1910, he joined the RAMC and served with great distinction in the 1914–18 War, winning the Military Cross and being three times mentioned in dispatches, besides being awarded the DSO in 1917. He retired in 1936 with the rank of Lieutenant-Colonel. On his retirement he moved with his family to Ham Court, Upton-on-Severn. This had been the stately home of the Martin family since the eighteenth century, and was sold by Major Eliot George Bromley-Martin in 1925. By then all but one wing had been pulled down, and this was occupied by a variety of people until the Pantons took it over. It was with their daughter Honor Mary Panton in Ham Court that Marie and Conway Lowe sought refuge in the early days of the Second World War.

What had happened was that an enemy plane, on its way back from a bombing mission in 1940–41, had dropped a stick of five incendiary bombs on Somerset Road, and glass and the contents of 'Eversley' were scattered everywhere. Though unhurt themselves, it was clearly time to move (Marie was 75 and Conway 81), and the obvious choice was to join forces with their daughter, Honor Mary Panton and family in the Worcestershire house where they had settled some years before. Marie and Conway stayed with the Pantons at Ham Court until nearly the end of the war; but in mid-1944 they moved to the Red House, Drayton, near Norwich, where Marie died in November 1944 and Conway died in March 1947.

Honor Mary and Henry Forbes Panton had one son, Richard Forbes Panton and one daughter, Elizabeth Ann Panton. Richard married Stella Mary Grayson; their children were a boy and a girl. Living in Malvern, Richard died in May 1985 and their son was tragically killed in a traffic accident four years later when he was a student at London University. Elizabeth Ann Panton, the daughter of Honor Mary and Henry Forbes Panton, married David Gibson, whose career as an engineer took them to Burma and Malaysia. They had five children, three boys and two girls, and on their return to England settled in Woking.

Marie and Conway's second daughter, Joyce Burman Lowe, married Humphrey Richard Owen Drake. He completed his civil service career as an inspector in the Ministry of Agriculture and Fisheries. As his wife had borne no children, they adopted a boy who became Roger Conway Drake and married. Marie and Conway's surviving son, Henry Conway Lowe (known in the family as Darby) married; he and his wife had no children. Darby, after farming and working as a land agent, trained as a Braille instructor. He was, by all accounts, a very caring person, and the fact that he himself suffered from a speech impediment may well have influenced him in taking up this work helping those with another form of handicap. He died in August 1978 and is survived by his widow, Jean Margaret Lowe.

(4) *Her grand-daughter's memories of Marie*

Mrs Elizabeth Ann Gibson very kindly agreed to contribute the following:

> The name Granny Lowe conjures up many magical memories for me. She was the head of a large family, a true matriarch in a large home in Birmingham—I was the youngest grandchild. Her strength of purpose was the backbone of the family—Grandfather Lowe never recovered from the tragedy of his eldest son's death. Uncle Dick was killed in the trenches in 1916—a brilliant young man, a Winchester Scholar, an Oxford University Scholar and destined for the Church. Granny Lowe's courage, deep faith and love and sense of duty supported the family. She was respected and deeply loved by all.
>
> My memory of her was that of a tall imposing lady always dressed in long dark flowing clothes; and she wore large hats whenever she went out of the house even in the garden. She was adventurous and full of fun and at the same time a strict Victorian—she always called Grandfather's greatest friend Harold Rayner by his surname, Mr Rayner. I knew her well as I lived with her when my parents were in India. She would 'phone the chauffeur Johnson from the breakfast table to order the car and we would go out to buy Kunzle Cakes for tea, or to the outfitter, Parkers, to buy clothes for me which were several sizes too large for me to grow into!
>
> It was not all pleasure. Granny was a realist and a great welfare worker. The latter was evident in her organisation of the Birmingham ladies to form a laundry during the 1914–18 War looking after the needs of the troops. Johnson the chauffeur was asked to drive us to other parts of Birmingham, to the poorer area where the Sewing Lady lived or to the row of narrow houses packed together where Nanny Favill lived. Granny wished me to see the world, not just 22 Somerset Road, Edgbaston. She thought of others, never of herself, and she combined great self-discipline with a gentle loving nature. I was aware of all this as a child as I had time to observe—I was to speak when I was spoken to and never to

speak out of turn. Discipline was strict for my brother Richard and me—we were terrified of Grandfather who administered it; reprimands from our much-loved Granny caused us grave concern.

I was of course unaware of the contents of this diary, particularly about her artistic ability and interest. We heard her play the piano but never the banjo. She could also yodel which was rather 'avant garde' for her time. Her deep interest in others appears in her diary and her thoughts were always of others before herself. I saw her go up the stepladder to hang the summer curtains in case May, the parlourmaid, fell and hurt herself!

Granny was bombed out of Birmingham and lived with us, exchanging a large house with servants for one room in a country house with no servants. She was well known in the village and wonderful in the way she managed the change of lifestyle with such resilience. She died when I was 17 years old. By that time I had realised how much she meant to all the family as well as me.

Granny was a truly wonderful character, exerting an influence for good and happiness all around by giving of herself and her love to everyone, and being such a support with her strength and wisdom. She was deeply loved and respected by all who knew her from every walk of life.